Only heaven will reveal how our children grew strong in the Lord through the influence of our prayers! But how should a parent pray for their little one? How can we engage in spiritual warfare on behalf of the boys and girls under our charge? Fern Nichols does an excellent job of bidding us into her circle of prayer with her excellent book, *Mom's Little Book of Powerful Prayers*. Believe me, it's anything but child's play—you hold in your hands a manual on how to partner with God in his grand design for your children!

Joni Eareckson Tada
Joni and Friends International Disability Center

This powerful, practical book gives straightforward and simple guidance for praying the heart of the Father and resting all your confidence on the power of his Word. You will find that nothing faces you or your children about which God has not given powerful promises. Marinate in his Word and let his Word be the mold in which your prayers are shaped.

Jennifer Kennedy Dean
Executive Director, The Praying Life Foundation,
author of *Live a Praying Life*

Also by Fern Nichols

Moms in Prayer

MOM'S LITTLE BOOK
of POWERFUL
PRAYERS

FERN NICHOLS

with Stephen and Amanda Sorenson

ZONDERVAN®

ZONDERVAN

Mom's Little Book of Powerful Prayers
Copyright © 2014 by Fern Nichols

This title is also available as a Zondervan ebook. Visit www.zondervan.com/ebooks.

Requests for information should be addressed to:
Zondervan, 3900 Sparks Dr., Grand Rapids, Michigan 49546

Library of Congress Cataloging-in-Publication Data

Nichols, Fern, 1945–

    Mom's little book of powerful prayers / Fern Nichols with Stephen and Amanda Sorenson.
        pages cm
    Includes index.
    ISBN 978-0-310-33762-1 (softcover)
    1. Mothers—Prayers and devotions. 2. Prayer—Christianity. 3. Bible—Devotional
use. I. Sorenson, Stephen. II. Sorenson, Amanda, 1953– III. Title.
BV283.M7 N53—2014
242'.8431—dc23
                                         2013037387

Published in association with the literary agency of Ann Spangler and Company, 1420 Pontiac Road SE, Grand Rapids, MI 49506.

Cover design: Thinkpen Design
Imagery: iStockphoto
Interior design: Katherine Lloyd, The DESK

Printed in the United States of America

16 17 18 /OPP/ 23 22 21 20 19 18 17 16 15 14 13 12 11 10 9 8 7 6 5 4

contents

To my faithful, loving heavenly Father,
who with great patience continues to teach me to pray.

To my daughter, Trisha,
and three daughters-in-love: Patti, Bonnie, and Tara,
who know the power of God through personal and corpo-
rate prayer.
What great joy to this nana's heart
that you are praying daily for my grandchildren.
I am extremely grateful to God
that you are walking in the prayers
of those who came before you.

A Letter to Moms

Dear Mom,

I know it's not easy raising children today. So many influences and ideas fight to capture our children's hearts. I have four married children and eight grandchildren, and my concerns for their spiritual, emotional, intellectual, relational, and physical well-being are great. I welcome Jesus' invitation: "Come to me, all you who are weary and burdened, and I will give you rest" (Matthew 11:28). It is a promise I'm glad I can count on.

Having the opportunity to talk about these concerns with my heavenly Father gives me hope when I feel hopeless, peace when I am fearful, and wisdom when I don't know what to do. That is why I'm sharing this little prayer book with you. I have experienced the love of a faithful God who hears and answers my prayers, and I want you to have that experience too.

There is nothing — absolutely nothing — of concern to us that God does not care about. Our concerns are his concerns. He says, "Call on me in the day of trouble; I will deliver you, and you will honor me" (Psalm 50:15). Nothing is too little or too big to share with God in prayer. We can pray about every need our children have.

When we place our children's needs in God's hands through prayer, we call forth his intervention, blessing, and protection. So prayer is not only a wonderful gift to give our children; it's a powerful antidote to the fears and worries that often accompany motherhood. I am excited for you to begin this journey as an intercessor for your children by standing in the gap and praying for their needs. I know these prayers have the power to be life changing for you and your children.

The prayers in this book follow a specific pattern, beginning with the Scripture chosen for each prayer need. Scripture is what makes the prayers so powerful. When we pray God's Word, we are praying God's heart. When we place our children's names into Scripture, we are praying back to God his will for our children. I'm thankful for the reassurance that I can trust God to be true to his Word: "For with God nothing is ever impossible and no word from God shall be without power or impossible of fulfillment" (Luke 1:37 AMP).

The prayers also include praise, confession, and thanks. These are important for preparing our hearts to intercede for our children. The praise focuses our attention on one of God's attributes. It helps enlarge our vision of who God is, which leads us to greater trust of the God we know. Confession helps make us aware of any sin that would block our communication with God and reminds us that whatever virtue we are praying for our children, we need to model ourselves, and whatever weakness we want to discourage in our children, we also need God's help to discourage in ourselves. Thanksgiving helps open our hearts to magnify the Lord for what he has done and anticipate what he will do.

Because these prayers are based on the timeless truths of Scripture, you should find them suitable for all ages and stages — for young children, teens, and even for adult children. For the sake of simplicity, I have written each prayer for a male or female child, but nearly all of the prayers are applicable for either gender, so pray them according to your child's identity. Because our times bring unique challenges often not faced by previous generations, I have included a number of prayers on contemporary topics or issues, including, for example, body image, social media, mental illness, and divorce, to name a few. No matter what you or your child might be facing, be assured that God's Word will address the problem and bring much-needed comfort and wisdom.

Feel free to use these prayers sequentially as they appear in the book, or use the index to choose prayers according to your child's need at the moment. However you proceed, I encourage you to take your time. Resist the temptation to pray hastily. Allow God's Spirit to mold your heart to his will as you praise his character, confess your sin, and give him thanks. May these prayers be a springboard to a lifelong journey of intercessory prayer for your child. May they inspire prayers for many more needs — not just for your child, but for this whole generation of children.

My prayer for you, precious mom, is that these prayers will cultivate a closer, more intimate, loving relationship with your heavenly Father. You are his beloved child, and he longs to hear your voice. Whether God says yes, no, or wait, he will be faithful to hear and answer your prayers.

Rest assured that your prayers are powerful and effective; they make a difference. You will never regret the time you invest in prayer. Prayer is a legacy you can give your children that will last forever.

May God bless you and your children,
Fern

HOW TO KNOW THAT GOD WILL HEAR YOUR PRAYERS

Just as a mom recognizes the voice of her own child, our heavenly Father knows the voice of each of his children. If you have a question or doubt concerning your personal relationship with God, let me share with you how you can be certain you are his child.

There is one unchangeable truth you can count on: God loves you personally! In his great love, he gave the world his greatest treasure — his only Child, Jesus Christ. Jesus died on the cross in your place as payment for your sins and for the sins of the whole world. Because of his death and resurrection, you can experience God's indescribable love, both now and throughout all eternity.

No matter where your sins have taken you, God's forgiveness is perfect and complete because of Jesus' sacrifice. Will you take your first step of faith by recognizing that you need forgiveness for your sins and believing that Jesus died for you? If you ask for his forgiveness and accept him as your Savior and Lord, you will never be the same. He will replace your loneliness, fears, frustrations, and guilt with his love and forgiveness. He also promises to hear your prayers and answer them with all the delight of an earthly parent responding to the desires of a beloved child.

Make the following prayer the first and most important prayer of your life:

Dear Father, thank you for sending your Son, Jesus, to die on the cross for my sin. I want to be your child. Please come into my heart and forgive all my sins. I want to live for you alone. Thank you for making my heart your home. In Jesus' name, amen.

If you have prayed this prayer, you are a member of God's family. God promises, "To all who did receive him, to those who believed in his name, he gave the right to become children of God" (John 1:12). You are his child! You can know for sure that God will hear and answer your prayers.

Welcome to the family of God!

Prayers

For My Child to Receive God's Gift of Salvation

> God so loved the world that he gave his one and only Son, that whoever believes in him shall not perish but have eternal life. (John 3:16)

Praise God: For he is love.

Confess: Any tendency to question God's love for me or my children.

Offer Thanks: For loving me with an unchanging, unconditional love that has no limits.

Ask God: Loving heavenly Father, I pray that my child will believe this truth: God so loved the world that he gave his one and only Son, that whoever believes in him shall not perish but have eternal life. I pray that in your great mercy, you will draw my son close to your heart so that he will experience your unconditional love and realize he is a sinner who needs a Savior. Reveal to him that you loved him so much, you made forgiveness of his sin possible through the shed blood of Christ on the cross. Open his spiritual eyes to see your marvelous love. I ask that he would respond by repenting of his sin and asking you into his heart. Father, I implore you to save my son to love and serve you faithfully all the days of his life. May he know complete forgiveness — that he is part of your forever family, and nothing would ever cause you to withdraw your love from him. In the name of my loving Jesus I pray, amen.

Remember: God showed his perfect love by sending Jesus our Savior to die for us.

Uniquely Created
to Do Good Things

We are God's masterpiece. He has created us anew in Christ
Jesus, so that we can do the good things he planned for us long
ago. (Ephesians 2:10 NLT)

Praise God: Who is our creator.

Confess: Any lack of appreciation for the unique people God
has created my children to be.

Offer Thanks: That God created us anew in Christ so that we
may fulfill the good things he has planned.

Ask God: Creator God, I ask for my child to understand that
she is your masterpiece, created anew in Christ Jesus so that
she can do the good things you planned for her long ago. O
Father, you never make mistakes — not one. May my precious
daughter know how wonderfully perfect you made her. May
she rejoice in the gifts, abilities, and talents you gave uniquely
to her. She truly is your masterpiece. I pray that she would
compare herself with no one else and would not strive to imi-
tate anyone else or try to do what they do. There is no one who
can glorify you the same way she can. Please give me wisdom
to fulfill my role in encouraging her to be who she is in Christ
and in helping her develop the gifts and talents you have given
her. In the name of Jesus, amen.

Remember: God, our Father, is our perfect, loving creator.

Love:
The Fruit of God's Spirit

When the Holy Spirit controls our lives, he will produce this kind of fruit in us: love. (Galatians 5:22 NLT 1996)

Praise God: For his measureless love.

Confess: Any resistance to the Holy Spirit's work in my life or lack of true love in my relationships.

Offer Thanks: For the Holy Spirit who works tirelessly to reproduce God's love in us.

Ask God: Eternal, loving God, I pray that the Holy Spirit will control my child's life, producing the fruit of love. Please reveal your unconditional love to him — the selfless, sacrificial love that Christ displayed on the cross when he gave himself to forgive the sins of the whole world. Reproduce your love in his life, empowering him through your Holy Spirit to love the unlovely, to be kind and gentle, and to be unselfish and giving. When people come into his life who truly annoy and irritate him or say hurtful things to or about him, may he promptly ask for your help in loving them as he loves himself. By the power of the Holy Spirit who lives in him, cultivate the fruit of love in his life so that others may know he belongs to you. In Jesus' name, amen.

Remember: God is perfect love.

To Experience
God's Forgiveness

In [Jesus] we have redemption through his blood, the forgiveness of sins. (Ephesians 1:7)

Praise God: That he is our God who forgives.

Confess: Any reluctance to seek forgiveness or any belief that God won't forgive.

Offer Thanks: For God's forgiving heart and the blood of Jesus that washes clean our sins and sets us free from the guilt of sin.

Ask God: My God who forgives, I ask that in Jesus, my child would have redemption through his blood, the forgiveness of sins. I pray that she will not hesitate to come to you in confession and repentance. May she find rest and peace in the mercy of your forgiveness. Help her understand that your forgiveness is immediate and complete — no matter how undeserving she may be. Touch her heart to know how much your unconditional love completely forgives. May she find comfort in the assurance that your boundless forgiveness keeps no record of her past sins. In Jesus' name, amen.

Remember: God is merciful, patient, and faithful to forgive.

Self-Esteem
for a Child of God

To all who received [Jesus], to those who believed in his name,
he gave the right to become children of God. (John 1:12)

Praise God: That he is our loving Father.

Confess: Any lingering doubt that God loves me or that I am his precious child.

Offer Thanks: That through the blood of Jesus, God gave me the right to become his child.

Ask God: O Abba Father, in your grace you drew my child to your heart and gave her the right to become your child by believing in your name and receiving you. By your grace, help her understand what being your child really means: that she is dearly and eternally loved; that she is your special treasure; that you have declared her perfect, precious, and honored in your sight; that you rejoice over her with singing; that your plans and purposes for her life are very good. O Father, by your grace help her to live in the confident assurance of how you see her — a greatly valued daughter of the King — and not to look for the approval and acceptance of others to build her self-esteem. Help me to be more intentional about reminding her how highly valued she is in my eyes as well. In Jesus' name, amen.

Remember: God is our loving Father, who longs to draw us to himself.

6

Trust God to Be a Refuge

The LORD is good, a refuge in times of trouble. He cares for those who trust in him. (Nahum 1:7)

Praise God: That he is our refuge.

Confess: Any tendency to allow uncertainties and problems to overwhelm my mind and lead me to doubt God's goodness.

Offer Thanks: To God, my refuge, who is always good and expresses his goodness in so many caring ways.

Ask God: God my refuge, I pray that my child will believe that you are good and are a refuge in times of trouble. May she know that you care for those who trust in you. She is having a hard time and is trying to handle her problems all on her own. I pray that she will not be afraid to relinquish control, that she will entrust to your care her desires, expectations, and troubled heart. Help her believe your promise that no matter how dark the situation seems, everything will work out for her good. Please restore her joy as she takes refuge in the promise that you care for her. In Jesus' name, amen.

Remember: Even when we are in crisis, we can trust God to be our refuge.

Gaining Confidence that God Hears and Answers Prayer

This is the confidence we have in approaching God: that if we ask anything according to his will, he hears us. And if we know that he hears us — whatever we ask — we know that we have what we asked of him. (1 John 5:14–15)

Praise God: Who hears.

Confess: My arrogance when I pursue my own way instead of humbly seeking God and his will in my life.

Offer Thanks: For God's listening ear and his faithfulness in answering my prayers.

Ask God: O Father who hears, I ask that you would place in my child's heart this confidence in approaching you: that if he asks anything according to your will, you hear him. And if he knows that you hear him — whatever he asks — may he also know that he will have what he asks of you. Increase his faith and build in him a strong belief in your promise that because he is your child, he can approach you with confidence. I ask that your words would dwell richly in my child so he will ask according to your will. Grant him patience as he awaits your answer. In Jesus' name, amen.

Remember: God, who hears and answers prayer, is faithful to keep all his promises.

Choosing to Trust God's Plan

"For I know the plans I have for you," declares the LORD, "plans to prosper you and not to harm you, plans to give you hope and a future." (Jeremiah 29:11)

Praise God: Who is sovereign.

Confess: The times when circumstances overwhelm me, leading me to doubt and lose hope in the good work God is accomplishing in my life.

Offer Thanks: That our sovereign God's plans cannot be thwarted by any power, person, or circumstance.

Ask God: O sovereign Lord, blessed controller of all things, I pray that my child might know the plans you have for him: plans to prosper him and not to harm him, plans to give him a hope and a future. May this truth be his confidence and sweet peace throughout his life's journey. I ask that you would grant him a clear conviction of your unconditional love, because you personally scheduled each day of his life before he began to breathe. O Lord, may he live daily in your sovereign plan, trusting you without hesitation. In Jesus' name, amen.

Remember: God is sovereign, giving us hope for the future.

To Be Encouraged
by God's Protective Presence

You are a shield around me, O LORD; you bestow glory on me and lift up my head. (Psalm 3:3)

Praise God: Who is our shield.

Confess: Any lack of focus on God's faithfulness that leads to feelings of being consumed or defeated by the circumstances of life.

Offer Thanks: For the times I have experienced God's protective shield around me or my family.

Ask God: O Divine Shield, I pray for you to be a shield around my child. Bestow glory on him and lift up his head. Please come alongside him through the power of your Holy Spirit and change his "I cannot" to "I can." May he find hope and encouragement through your Word. I pray that when he feels vulnerable or fearful, you will reveal your presence as a protective shield around him. May he know that every day is full of hope because of his faithful God. If his head is downcast because of his sins, I pray that he will humble himself and ask for forgiveness. I ask that he would feel your faithful touch lifting his head once again. In Jesus' name, amen.

Remember: God Almighty is our shield, Savior, and deliverer.

Strength to Pursue Righteousness

May [the Lord] strengthen your hearts so that you will be blame-less and holy in the presence of our God and Father when our Lord Jesus comes with all his holy ones. (1 Thessalonians 3:13)

Praise God: That he is righteous.

Confess: Any times when my heart pursues things that do not belong in God's holy presence.

Offer Thanks: That God is righteous, faithful to watch over us in all our ways.

Ask God: O righteous God and Father, I pray that you will strengthen my child's heart so he will be blameless and holy in your presence when the Lord Jesus comes with all his holy ones. Fill my son with your Holy Spirit so he might hunger and thirst for righteousness. I ask that he would want his every thought, word, and deed to be righteous, true, honorable, pure, and pleasing to you. I pray that he will walk blamelessly before you his whole life, bringing you glory. In Jesus' power-ful name, amen.

Remember: God our Father is perfect and holy in righteousness.

To Pursue Godly Virtues

Pursue righteousness, godliness, faith, love, endurance and gentleness. Fight the good fight of the faith. (1 Timothy 6:11–12)

Praise God: Who is pure.

Confess: Any lack of diligence in pursuing the righteousness and faith to which God calls me.

Offer Thanks: That our pure God gives us everything we need to fight the good fight of the faith.

Ask God: O pure God, I pray that my child will pursue righteousness, godliness, faith, love, endurance, and gentleness so that he may fight the good fight of the faith. May his walk be strengthened through the study of your Word, and may he uphold it as the standard for his life. Through the power of your Word, arm him to be a mighty warrior of faith. Open his spiritual eyes to see all things today in light of eternity, and make him a good witness for Christ as he lives out godly virtues. I pray that growing in faith will be his main priority. In Jesus' powerful name, amen.

Remember: God is pure, righteous, loving, and gentle.

Strength to
Choose Right from Wrong

It is God who arms me with strength and makes my way perfect.
(2 Samuel 22:33)

Praise God: Who is our strength.

Confess: Any dependence on my own resources and strength instead of relying on God and the strength he so generously gives.

Offer Thanks: To God for strengthening those who ask for it.

Ask God: O Lord my strength, I pray that my child would know that you arm her with strength and make her way perfect. Through the power of your Spirit, strengthen her heart to choose your ways according to your Word. Make her path straight as she faces daily choices between right and wrong. With your help, may she live a righteous life, desiring to please you by obeying your commands. May she experience the joy of obeying you, understanding that she can do good only through your strength. In Jesus' name, amen.

Remember: Nothing can stand against the strength of our mighty God.

Desire a Teachable Spirit

Teach me to do your will, for you are my God; may your good
Spirit lead me on level ground. (Psalm 143:10)

Praise God: For he is our teacher.

Confess: Any unwillingness to learn or resistance to doing
God's will.

Offer Thanks: For the times God has taught me to do his will
and led me in his perfect ways.

Ask God: God my teacher, I pray that you will teach my child
to do your will, for you are her God. May your good Spirit lead
her on level ground. I pray that your words will always ring
true in her mind. I ask you to fill her with your Holy Spirit
and guide her in your truth. Grant her a teachable spirit that
willingly learns your ways. Help her to humbly receive your
great knowledge, and may she not be stubborn or rebellious,
refusing your counsel. I also ask that she would be attentive
to and not refuse the godly counsel of others. May she desire
to bring you honor and glory throughout her life. Please give
me wisdom in teaching her your truth and leading her in your
ways. In Jesus' name, amen.

Remember: God is a trustworthy teacher who leads us in his
perfect ways.

Help for
Struggles with Schoolwork

I am the LORD, your God, who takes hold of your right hand and says to you, Do not fear; I will help you. (Isaiah 41:13)

Praise God: That he is our helper.

Confess: Any pride or doubt that keeps me from admitting my need for help or accepting help when it is offered.

Offer Thanks: For the times God my helper has come to my aid.

Ask God: O Lord my helper, I pray that my child will know that you are the Lord his God, who takes hold of his right hand and says to him, "Do not fear; I will help you." May the promise of your words reassure him as he struggles with his studies at school. Please give his teachers patience, compassion, and wisdom to know how to help him learn. I pray that he will not be too proud or embarrassed to ask his teacher for help, and may he be eager to ask for your help as well. When he calls on you, give him an understanding of his lessons, enlighten his mind, and protect him from discouragement. Grant him peace and contentment when he knows that he has tried his best. In Jesus' name, amen.

Remember: God is always our helper.

Having Confidence in God's Gifts of Talent and Ability

God is able to make all grace abound to you, so that in all things at all times, having all that you need, you will abound in every good work. (2 Corinthians 9:8)

Praise God: That he is gracious.

Confess: Any tendency to procrastinate, despair, or give up because of feelings of inadequacy.

Offer Thanks: That my gracious God has uniquely gifted my child.

Ask God: My gracious Father, I ask that your grace would abound to my child so that in all things at all times, having all that she needs, she will abound in every good work. Lord, my child doubts her talents and abilities. She feels incapable and lacks confidence. I pray for your grace to be upon her life so that she will be grateful for and excel in the abilities you have given her. Protect her from the harm and damage of comparing herself with others. O Lord, help her recognize that you have uniquely created her with special gifts and talents to do the good work you have planned for her. Help me as a mother to recognize her abilities, and grant me your wisdom to know how to nurture and encourage her. In Jesus' name, amen.

Remember: God, our gracious Father, will provide all that we need.

Using Time Wisely

Teach us to number our days aright, that we may gain a heart of wisdom. (Psalm 90:12)

Praise God: For he is eternal.

Confess: Any moments spent wasting precious time on things that really don't matter.

Offer Thanks: For the challenges, adventures, and discoveries of each new day that provide an opportunity to serve and honor our eternal God.

Ask God: O blessed, eternal God, I ask that you would teach my child to number his days aright, that he may gain a heart of wisdom. I pray that above all things, he will seek you first, for the fear of the Lord is the beginning of wisdom. The wise man builds his life on the truths of your Word; may this be true of my child. Help him to be self-disciplined and diligent, with a keen sense of responsibility in the use of his time, and give me wisdom as I guide him in the many choices of activities and demands upon his time. By your grace and with eternity in mind, help us use the wisdom and time you have given us so that we would bring honor and glory to you. In Jesus' name, amen.

Remember: God is eternal, teaching us to number our days aright.

To Experience the
Healthy Effects of Trusting God

Trust in the LORD with all your heart and lean not on your own understanding; in all your ways acknowledge him, and he will make your paths straight. Do not be wise in your own eyes; fear the LORD and shun evil. This will bring health to your body and nourishment to your bones. (Proverbs 3:5–8)

Praise God: That he is the giver of life.

Confess: Any burdens I carry that take the joy out of life and leave my body broken and depleted because I am trusting in my own wisdom instead of God's.

Offer Thanks: For the power and nourishment of God's life-giving words.

Ask God: O Father, Giver of Life, I pray that my child will trust in you with all her heart and lean not on her own understanding. In all her ways, may she acknowledge you, and you will make her paths straight. May she not be wise in her own eyes but fear you and shun evil. Thank you for the promise that this will bring health to her body and nourishment to her bones. Father, so many harmful things could damage her body and her mind. I pray against anything that might bring ill health to her body, to her mental state, and ultimately to her soul. Protect her from yielding to temptation. May she have a reverent fear of you, Lord, and desire only to please you. I pray that she will enjoy good health in body and mind so that she might serve you with great zeal all the days of her life. In Jesus' name, amen.

Remember: Our God is the giver of life, who satisfies the hunger of our hearts.

A Desire to Be Attractive

You created my inmost being; you knit me together in my mother's womb. I praise you because I am fearfully and wonderfully made; your works are wonderful, I know that full well. (Psalm 139:13–14)

Praise God: Exalt God, the creator of all things.

Confess: Any times I have taken for granted the awesome works of God's hands or not appreciated who he created me to be.

Offer Thanks: That God marvelously and uniquely created each of us in our mothers' wombs and declared his work good.

Ask God: O blessed Creator, you created my child's inmost being; you knit her together in the womb. May she praise you because she is fearfully and wonderfully made and know full well that your works are wonderful. I am very concerned because she thinks she is not attractive enough and wants to change her outward appearance. O Father, please help her know that you do not make mistakes; you uniquely designed her for a specific purpose, and she is beautiful in your eyes. May this truth sink deep into her soul. Enable her to change the things she can and be at peace with the things she can't. Please help me model a balanced Christian perspective on self-image, clothing, and care of the body. Renew our minds in your truth. Remind us that reflecting the beauty of Christ is far more important than our outward appearance. In Jesus' name, amen.

Remember: God our Father and creator made us wonderful in his sight.

A Need for God's Healing

I am the LORD, who heals you. (Exodus 15:26)

Praise God: Who is the Great Physician.

Confess: Any times I have doubted God's compassion and willingness to heal.

Offer Thanks: To our Great Physician for his power to heal our afflictions, great and small.

Ask God: O blessed Great Physician, you are the Lord who heals. I ask you to heal my child. By the power of your great mercy, provide strength as he fights the daily challenges of this illness. Help him to be courageous and not become discouraged. I pray for your healing power to touch his body so that he will enjoy good health once again. During this time of sickness, I ask you to strengthen his inner spirit and make him more like Jesus. Please use this affliction to help him become a more compassionate, caring person who is quick to pray for others who are sick. I ask that you would grant the doctors wisdom, understanding, and compassion in treating my child. Please help him sleep peacefully knowing that he is in the palm of your hand and that you will never leave him or forsake him. In Jesus' name, amen.

Remember: God, our Great Physician, is kind, compassionate, and merciful.

A Need for God's Protection

I will take refuge in the shadow of your wings until the disaster has passed. (Psalm 57:1)

Praise God: For he is a sure refuge.

Confess: The times I seek my own solutions and go my own way when I feel threatened.

Offer Thanks: That even though the storms of life may come, I can find peace, safety, and comfort within the protective embrace of God's presence.

Ask God: Dear Lord, my sure refuge, I pray that my child will take refuge in the shadow of your wings until the disaster has passed. You know the circumstances and situations, the places and people that cause my child to feel at risk. When she feels threatened, I pray that she will take refuge under your outstretched wings until the danger subsides. I trust you, Lord, to meet her at the center of these fearful places and situations. May you always be the one she runs to first. Spread your wings, Lord, and cover and protect my dear child. In Jesus' name, amen.

Remember: God is our secure refuge and protector.

A Longing for Acceptance

[God has] made us accepted in the Beloved. (Ephesians 1:6 NKJV)

Praise God: Who is our beloved.

Confess: The times I lose focus on how much my heavenly Father loves and accepts me.

Offer Thanks: That God chose me to be his beloved child.

Ask God: Dear beloved Father, I ask that my child would know that by your grace she has been accepted in your beloved Son, Jesus. Lord, it tears my heart to see my child feeling rejected, insecure, and unloved. She often says, "I'm never going to be good enough. Why would anyone want to like me?" I ask that she will know how much you love her. Father, you loved her so much that you gave your life for her — there is no greater love than that. Deliver her from any doubts concerning this truth. I pray that my child will believe with her heart, not just her mind, that you love her completely. May she find significance and acceptance because she is your beloved. In Jesus' name, amen.

Remember: God is our beloved Father, who loves us more than we can imagine.

Choosing Friends Carefully

He who walks with the wise grows wise, but a companion of fools suffers harm. (Proverbs 13:20)

Praise God: Who is our friend.

Confess: Any unwise relationships I have chosen.

Offer Thanks: To Jesus for being the perfect friend who fills my lonely heart forever.

Ask God: Dear God, my friend, I ask you to help my child walk with the wise so that he will grow wise. Protect him from being a companion of fools so that he won't suffer harm. Give him spiritual discernment in choosing his friends. May he come to understand that the foundation of friendship is unconditional love — the kind of love you have for him. Please provide at least one Christian friend for my child so that together they can encourage each other's faith, be strong in godly character, and make godly decisions. I also pray for the salvation of his friends who are lost without Christ. In Jesus' name, amen.

Remember: God is our wise and faithful friend.

Forgiving Others

Be kind and compassionate to one another, forgiving each other,
just as in Christ God forgave you. (Ephesians 4:32)

Praise God: Who forgives.

Confess: Any bitterness or thoughts of retaliation toward anyone who has hurt me deeply.

Offer Thanks: To God for his saving grace that gives us compassion and kindness to forgive those we need to forgive.

Ask God: O forgiving God, I pray for my child to be kind and compassionate to others, forgiving them just as in Christ you forgave her. She is having a hard time forgiving someone. She has been deeply hurt and is holding a grudge. I ask you to replace her spirit of bitterness with your spirit of forgiveness. May she extend to the one who has offended her the same compassion and forgiveness that you have given her. I ask that your love will abound in her life, giving her strength to rid herself of this enslavement of an unforgiving spirit. May she experience victory and freedom — the fruit of forgiveness. In Jesus' precious name I pray, amen.

Remember: God is faithful to forgive; he is compassionate and kind.

To Honor One's Parents

Children, obey your parents in the Lord, for this is right. "Honor your father and mother" — which is the first commandment with a promise — "that it may go well with you and that you may enjoy long life on the earth." (Ephesians 6:1–3)

Praise God: Who is our Father.

Confess: Any times I dishonor my parents by my thoughts, words, or actions.

Offer Thanks: To God for being an awesome Father who teaches us how to enjoy life on earth.

Ask God: Heavenly Father, my prayer for my child is that he will obey his parents in the Lord, for this is right. May he honor us so that as you have promised, it may go well with him, and he may enjoy long life on this earth. Help us as his parents to be good examples of faithful obedience to you, modeling respect, kindness, and gentleness to our own aging parents. Please give our child an eager and willing heart that is open to accepting guidance and direction from us. Help him see that we, as your chosen representatives, are responsible to lead, guide, and give him instruction in living a life that honors you. Grant us the wisdom and love we need to correct and train our child in your ways. May he heed our instruction and learn from our correction. Please give him a heart that wants to please us and you. In Jesus' name, amen.

Remember: God is our heavenly Father, who keeps all of his promises.

Choosing the Right "Hero"

Jesus ... said, "I am the light of the world. Whoever follows me will never walk in darkness, but will have the light of life." (John 8:12)

Praise God: Who is the Light of the World.

Confess: Any time I am tempted to follow anyone but Jesus.

Offer Thanks: That God sent his Son, a trustworthy guide to light the path ahead.

Ask God: O Divine Light, I praise you for your perfect Son, Jesus, who is the Light of the World. May my child follow you and never walk in darkness but have the light of life. Jesus is the perfect light for my child to look up to and follow. I pray that she will choose Jesus to be her hero so that she will never walk in darkness. May her heart long to be like you: kind, compassionate, honest, forgiving, and full of love. I pray that she would choose earthly role models who reflect your nature. May she pledge allegiance to you, her Lord and Savior, and take pride in being called your child. I pray that you will always be her number-one role model. In Jesus' name, amen.

Remember: Jesus is the Light of the World, and his light brings life.

Delight in Having a Servant's Heart

Each one should use whatever gift he has received to serve
others, faithfully administering God's grace in its various forms.
(1 Peter 4:10)

Praise God: Who is a servant.

Confess: The many times I put my selfish desires and ambitions above the opportunity to administer God's grace to others.

Offer Thanks: That God the Son humbled himself to take on the limitations and poverty of humanity and become the servant of all.

Ask God: O Servant Lord, I ask that my child would use whatever gift he has received to serve others, faithfully administering your grace in its various forms. Teach him to do nothing out of selfish ambition or vain conceit, but to humbly consider others before himself. Let him look not only to his own interests but also to the interests of others. I ask that he would be sensitive to the needs of those around him. Allow him to encourage those who are downcast and rejoice with those who succeed. I pray that he will serve others with a humble attitude, not one of superiority. Help me to be a good example of your servant heart — a model he can follow. In Jesus' name I pray, amen.

Remember: Our Lord God chose to be our servant.

A Dose of Courage, Please

Be strong and courageous. Do not be terrified; do not be discouraged, for the Lord your God will be with you wherever you go. (Joshua 1:9)

Praise God: For he is our ever-present God.

Confess: The times I am swayed by the circumstances and emotions of the moment and become fearful and discouraged.

Offer Thanks: That God is faithful to be present in my life, protecting me, strengthening me, and giving me courage.

Ask God: Dear ever-present God, I pray for my child to be strong and courageous. I pray that she will not be terrified or discouraged, for you, the Lord her God, will be with her wherever she goes. I ask that you would give her strength to face the things that cause panic in her heart. Give her courage to confront her mountains with confidence in the knowledge that through your mighty power, she can and will succeed. May she know that your presence is always with her. Help her look to you for courage to live victoriously according to your will. In Jesus' name, amen.

Remember: God is our ever-present Father.

Patience Will Be
Tested through Adversity

Be joyful in hope, patient in affliction, faithful in prayer.
(Romans 12:12)

Praise God: For he is patient.

Confess: Any impatience when people and circumstances don't fall in line with my timetable.

Offer Thanks: For God's faithful patience and forgiveness even when we are slow and stubborn in responding to him.

Ask God: O most patient Father, I ask that my child would be joyful in hope, patient in affliction, and faithful in prayer. May he be strengthened with all power, great endurance, and patience according to your glorious might. Father, thank you that he will mature in patience through the many trials and tests of his life. I trust that the testing of his faith will bring great endurance. May he wait patiently, trusting your promises and obeying your Word. Please give him a heart that perseveres and presses through the most difficult situations. May he keep his eyes on you, faithfully praying to the author and finisher of his faith. In Jesus' name, amen.

Remember: God is most patient, abounding in love, joy, and faithfulness.

Learning to Control Anger

Everyone should be quick to listen, slow to speak and slow to become angry, for man's anger does not bring about the righteous life that God desires. (James 1:19–20)

Praise God: For he is holy.

Confess: The harsh and biting words that spill out of my mouth before I can stop them, wounding whoever may be in my way.

Offer Thanks: To my holy God, whose merciful heart responds to anger with kind words of correction and restoration.

Ask God: O most holy God, may my child be quick to listen, slow to speak, and slow to become angry, for his anger does not bring about the righteous life that you desire. Please help him learn to be quick to listen to what others have to say. Teach him to be slow to speak, taking time to consider his words. And restrain his temper so that he will be slow to become angry when he is frustrated or irritated. Help him not to harbor anger but be quick to resolve his conflicts so that bitterness does not take root in his heart. Fill him with your wisdom so he will handle challenging situations in a loving and kind manner. Give him a heart of mercy and remind him that you have been merciful to him. In Jesus' name, amen.

Remember: We serve a holy God who is slow to anger.

Comfort for a Broken Heart

The LORD ... has sent me to bind up the brokenhearted ... to bestow on them a crown of beauty instead of ashes, the oil of gladness instead of mourning, and a garment of praise instead of a spirit of despair. (Isaiah 61:1, 3)

Praise God: That he is the God of all comfort.

Confess: Any doubt of God's faithful, compassionate, and merciful character.

Offer Thanks: For God's gifts of comfort that console the spirit and restore the joy of those who are worried, lonely, weary, sad, or discouraged.

Ask God: Blessed God of all comfort, I ask you to bind up my child's broken heart. Please bestow on him a crown of beauty instead of ashes, the oil of gladness instead of mourning, and a garment of praise instead of a spirit of despair. My heart aches to see my child carrying around hurts and frustrations that I can't fix. I wish I could, but only you, Lord, can heal him. Only you can be his joy and mend a heart that has been trampled. He needs your healing touch. Wipe away his tears and bring a song of joy back into his life. Turn my child's despair into praise. Let him experience your unfailing love so he can trust in your wise and perfect plan for his life. For your honor and glory, I pray in the name of Jesus, amen.

Remember: God is our comforter, who consoles, soothes, calms, reassures, and heals.

To Have a Caring, Compassionate Spirit

As God's chosen people, holy and dearly loved, clothe yourselves
with compassion, kindness, humility, gentleness and patience.
(Colossians 3:12)

Praise God: For he is compassionate.

Confess: Any times I am moved to tears by the suffering I see
and yet am not moved to respond with acts of compassion.

Offer Thanks: That God reveals his compassion not only in
word but also in deed.

Ask God: O compassionate Father, may my child, your chosen
son, holy and dearly loved, clothe himself with compassion,
kindness, humility, gentleness, and patience. I pray that he
would not be so self-absorbed that he overlooks the hurting
and wounded people around him. May he seize opportunities
to be caring and kind toward others. Motivate him toward
compassionate actions that will make a difference in his little
corner of the world. May he serve others with a heart that
overflows with compassion and draws them toward the heart
of Jesus. In Jesus' name, amen.

Remember: God is compassionate, kind, gentle, and patient.

The Lord Delivers
Us from Fear

I sought the LORD, and he answered me; he delivered me from all
my fears. Those who look to him are radiant; their faces are never
covered with shame. (Psalm 34:4–5)

Praise God: For he is our deliverer.

Confess: Any tendency to cling to fear, anxiety, or worry.

Offer Thanks: That God lifts the dark burden of fear from
those who look to him.

Ask God: Dear God, my deliverer, I ask that this will be said
of my child: that she sought you, and you answered her and
delivered her from all her fears. May her face be radiant and
never covered with shame, because she looks to you. Help
her know that you are able to deliver her from all her fears —
that your perfect love casts out fear. Help my child to rely on
the power of the Holy Spirit to provide the courage and faith
she needs to go forward. May she replace her fears with the
promises of your Word. Help her live in peace, trusting you.
In Jesus' name, amen.

Remember: God is our deliverer, our hope who delivers us
from fear.

Jesus Promises Freedom from Condemnation

There is now no condemnation for those who are in Christ Jesus. (Romans 8:1)

Praise God: Who is merciful.

Confess: Any belief that God is still angry with me for the sins he has already forgiven.

Offer Thanks: For God's merciful forgiveness that removes the guilt and penalty of sin.

Ask God: My merciful Lord, I ask that my child would know and experience this truth: There is now no condemnation for those who are in Christ Jesus. I pray that she will know beyond a shadow of doubt that Jesus paid for all her sins on the cross. If she is weighed down with guilt, I pray that this truth will penetrate her heart: if she has truly repented of her sin, she is forgiven no matter how she feels. Lord, your mercy sets her free from condemnation because you will never bring up her offenses again. Please help her forgive herself. In Jesus' name, amen.

Remember: We can trust our Father's merciful, compassionate, and forgiving heart.

The Desire to Be Like Jesus

We, who with unveiled faces all reflect the Lord's glory, are being transformed into his likeness with ever-increasing glory, which comes from the Lord, who is the Spirit. (2 Corinthians 3:18)

Praise God: For he is most holy.

Confess: Any impurity of thought or deed that veils the glory of God's character within me.

Offer Thanks: To God, who has given us the Holy Spirit to transform us into the likeness of Jesus.

Ask God: Dear most holy God, I pray that my child with unveiled face will reflect your glory, being transformed into your likeness with ever-increasing glory, which comes from the Lord, who is the Spirit. I know my son has been set apart to live a life worthy of you, bearing fruit in every good work. May his heart's desire be to please you. May he love the things you love. When he is tempted, I ask that he would draw on the strength and power of the Holy Spirit to help him do what is right. I pray that he will allow your Spirit to change him into your glorious likeness. In Jesus' name, amen.

Remember: Our God is holy, and by his Spirit, he transforms us into the likeness of his Son, Jesus Christ.

Knowing God through His Word

I want to know Christ and the power of his resurrection.
(Philippians 3:10)

Praise God: Who is our all-powerful God.

Confess: Any lack of desire or diligence in seeking to know Christ.

Offer Thanks: That God conquered death and invites us to know him through his Word.

Ask God: Omnipotent God, I ask that my child would want to know Christ and the power of his resurrection. I pray that he will turn away from the distractions of life and enter into the quietness of your presence. As he seeks to know you by reading your Word and praying, may he feel your love and sense your nearness. May the truths in your Word wash over his heart, bringing assurance of who he is in Christ. Open his spiritual eyes to experience your great power. May he love your words more than food and find them to be sweeter than honey. May he experience the joys and blessings of the abundant life you promise to those who know you. In Jesus' name, amen.

Remember: By his resurrection power, Christ is victorious over death.

Bad Company
Corrupts Good Character

Do not be misled: "Bad company corrupts good character."
Come back to your senses as you ought, and stop sinning.
(1 Corinthians 15:33–34)

Praise God: For he is our true friend.

Confess: Any tendency to seek out bad company.

Offer Thanks: That our holy God does not hide the truth from us.

Ask God: O God who is my friend, I pray that my child may not be misled: Bad company corrupts good character. Please, Lord, bring her back to her senses so that she will stop sinning. Open her eyes to see clearly how the company she keeps is leading her astray, taking her on a dark path away from your blessings. Make her restless, dissatisfied, and unhappy when she hangs out with these "friends." Give her courage to do what is right, even at the risk of being ridiculed or losing a friend. Father, please save those friends who need you so desperately, and bring other friends into her life who love and follow you. May my daughter desire to choose you as her best friend. For your glory, in the name of Jesus, amen.

Remember: God is our wise, forgiving, and true friend.

A Heart of Compassion

So, as those who have been chosen of God, holy and beloved,
put on a heart of compassion. (Colossians 3:12 NASB)

Praise God: Who is compassionate.

Confess: Any hardness of heart that does not reflect God's
holiness and love.

Offer Thanks: To God for his loving heart that overflows with
compassion for his beloved children.

Ask God: O compassionate Father, I thank you that my child
has been chosen of you and is holy and beloved. By your grace,
may she choose to put on a heart of compassion. Develop in
her a tender heart so that she will be known for her sympa-
thetic concern for people who are in distress or great need.
Reveal to her any self-absorbed tendencies that hinder her
from seeing those who are hurting and suffering. May she
be your hands and feet to those in need. May she grow each
day in reflecting your compassionate heart. And Lord, may
she see your compassionate heart reflected in me. In Jesus'
name, amen.

Remember: God is holy and compassionate.

Walking in Integrity

The man of integrity walks securely, but he who takes crooked paths will be found out. (Proverbs 10:9)

Praise God: Who is truth.

Confess: Any temptation to take shortcuts when it comes to integrity.

Offer Thanks: That God is the author and champion of integrity.

Ask God: O God of truth, I pray that my child will be a man of integrity who walks securely. I thank you that he will be found out if he takes a crooked path. By your grace, develop in him godly character that is single-minded in doing what is right. I pray that he will choose right paths as he follows you. May he be honest and keep his promises even when it hurts. Bless him with a clear conscience before you and others, and if he lies, may his conscience be so troubled that he immediately admits his wrong and repents. I pray that he would know the joy of being a person who can be trusted. And may he experience the freedom of not having to look over his shoulder in fear of the truth. For your glory, in Jesus' name, amen.

Remember: Our all-knowing God is perfect and true in all his ways.

To Have a Discerning Heart

So give your servant a discerning heart to govern your people and
to distinguish between right and wrong. (1 Kings 3:9)

Praise God: Who is all-wise.

Confess: Any times I ignore the nudging of my Spirit-filled
heart and choose what I know is wrong.

Offer Thanks: That God delivers us from bondage to sin and
by the truth of his Word empowers us to know right from
wrong.

Ask God: All-wise God, I pray that you will give my child
a discerning heart to govern your people and to distinguish
between right and wrong. Grant her a spirit of wisdom to make
good choices by knowing your Word and being sensitive to the
still, small voice of your Holy Spirit within her. Lord, instill
in her a determination to test everything by the truth of your
Word so that she will not be gullible or easily persuaded. If
she senses that what she is reading, hearing from her friends,
or being taught doesn't seem right, give her discernment to
see beyond the obvious to the hidden. As your disciple, may
she greatly influence the lives of others by helping them distinguish between right and wrong according to your Word.
Bless her greatly and use her mightily for your kingdom. In
Jesus' name, amen.

Remember: God is wise, and all his ways are righteous.

Choosing Friends Who Walk in God's Righteousness

Dear children, do not let anyone lead you astray. He who does what is right is righteous, just as [God] is righteous. (1 John 3:7)

Praise God: Who is our Good Shepherd.

Confess: Any inclination to be led astray by false values and to follow the ways and people of the world instead of obeying God.

Offer Thanks: To our Good Shepherd who leads us in righteousness and brings godly people into our lives.

Ask God: Good Shepherd, I ask that no one would lead my child astray. I pray that he will do what is right and seek to be righteous, just as you are righteous. Give him godly discernment in his choice of friends. I pray that he will not join the company of those who are bent on disobedience. May he influence his friends toward righteousness and not be open to any persuasive, ungodly influences. Father, he faces so much pressure from his peers. Help him to be strong in his convictions and courageous to stand alone, even if it means losing a friend. I ask you to give him your strength so he will be resolute in the face of opposition, but not self-righteous or offensive in his demeanor. I pray that he will be victorious in his faith by choosing to follow Jesus. In Jesus' name, amen.

Remember: God is our Good Shepherd, leading us in ways that are perfect.

A Plea for Sexual Purity

God wants you to be holy, so you should keep clear of all sexual sin. Then each of you will control your body and live in holiness and honor — not in lustful passion as the pagans do, in their ignorance of God and his ways. (1 Thessalonians 4:3–5 NLT 1996)

Praise God: For his holiness.

Confess: Any desire to turn away from God's ways and indulge in lustful passions.

Offer Thanks: That God teaches me how to walk in his ways.

Ask God: Holy Father, I cry out for my child that she would be holy and keep clear of all sexual sin. May she control her body and live in holiness and honor — not in lustful passion as the pagans do, in their ignorance of you and your ways. Help her say no to ungodly desires. Guard her mind from believing the lies that "everyone is doing it" and that your ways are old-fashioned. Bring godly influences into her life, and protect her from anyone who would lead her down an immoral path toward destruction. Give her the spiritual maturity to see that true love respects and honors you first. Empower her to stand firm and not give in to lustful passions. If she has fallen, may she repent and receive your forgiveness and healing. By the power of your Spirit, grant her self-control and keep her pure for her marriage bed. Keep her future husband pure as well, so their marriage may glorify you and be free from sexual baggage. In Jesus' name, amen.

Remember: God is holy, and his ways are true, bringing life to those who walk in them.

In Need of God's Wisdom

If any of you lacks wisdom, he should ask God, who gives generously to all without finding fault, and it will be given to him. (James 1:5)

Praise God: For his unsurpassed wisdom.

Confess: Any spirit of pride or independence that leads me to trust in my wisdom instead of seeking God's wisdom.

Offer Thanks: To God for sharing his wisdom with us.

Ask God: My all-knowing, wise God, you promise my child that if he lacks wisdom, he should ask you, who gives generously to all without finding fault, and it will be given to him. My child has come to a place where he does not know what to do, where to turn, or whom to ask for help. He is feeling alone and desperate. I pray that you would generously give him the wisdom he lacks. No matter how great or small his concern, may he know that he never bothers or offends you by asking. Please bring him to his knees to look up and call upon you. By your overwhelming love, grant him faith to believe that because you promised, he can count on receiving the wisdom he asks for. Use his trials to drive him to greater dependency on you. May going to you first for wisdom become a lifelong habit for him. In Jesus' name, amen.

Remember: God is generous and merciful in providing wisdom to those who ask.

To Live in Peace, Joy, and Hope

May the God of hope fill you with all joy and peace as you trust in him, so that you may overflow with hope by the power of the Holy Spirit. (Romans 15:13)

Praise God: Who is trustworthy.

Confess: Any lack of trust in God that empties me of peace, joy, and hope.

Offer Thanks: That we can have peace, joy, and hope because of who God is and what he gives to us.

Ask God: My trustworthy God of hope, I pray that you will fill my child with all joy and peace as she trusts in you, so that she may overflow with hope by the power of the Holy Spirit. Father, you came to give her an abundant life of joy, peace, and hope. Yet she is so prone to allowing circumstances to dictate her behavior and rob her of your precious gifts. Please guide her heart and mind to realize that joy, peace, and hope are not found in circumstances but in the person of Jesus Christ. May her reading of your Word and times in prayer be rich and satisfying, leading her to trust you for the peace, joy, and hope she longs for. Instill in her heart a deep, settled trust that you have everything under control. Lord, I pray that she may be filled with joy and hope by the power of your Holy Spirit so that peace might reign in her heart. In Jesus' name, amen.

Remember: God is our trustworthy source of joy, hope, and peace.

Being Kind and Forgiving to Siblings

Get rid of all bitterness, rage, anger, harsh words, and slander, as well as all types of evil behavior. Instead, be kind to each other, tenderhearted, forgiving one another, just as God through Christ has forgiven you. (Ephesians 4:31–32 NLT)

Praise God: Who is tenderhearted.

Confess: Any proclivity toward bitterness, rage, anger, harsh words, slander, or evil behavior.

Offer Thanks: For every tenderhearted kindness God has showered upon us.

Ask God: Tenderhearted Father, please help my children rid themselves of all bitterness, rage, anger, harsh words, slander, and evil behavior. May they be kind to each other, tenderhearted, forgiving one another, just as you through Christ have forgiven them. You see the conflict my children have with one another in our home. It breaks my heart that they treat each other so badly. Powerful God, I ask that you would intervene. It is not your will for them to hurt each other with disrespect, critical judgments, and harsh, unkind words. I pray boldly that you would put deep in their hearts a tenderhearted, forgiving love for each other. Give me the words to dispel the anger and encourage forgiveness. I ask that our home would have the sweet aroma of Christ. Give us victory for your name's sake, amen.

Remember: Our tenderhearted God is kind and forgiving, never malicious.

To Have a Faithful Heart

You are the LORD God, who chose Abram and … found his heart faithful to you. (Nehemiah 9:7–8)

Praise God: Who is faithful.

Confess: Any lack of faithfulness in trusting and obeying God.

Offer Thanks: That even when we are not faithful to God, he remains faithful to us.

Ask God: Dear faithful God, just as you chose Abraham and found his heart faithful, may my child's heart be found faithful to you as well. I pray that your character of faithfulness will be a quality he lives out every day of his life. May he be unwavering in his commitment to you and you alone. May he be a man of his word, determined to do what he says, and not just make a promise to give a good impression. May he steadfastly follow Jesus' example of being obedient to the Father's will. And when he sins and repents, Lord, may he have not one shred of doubt that you will be faithful to forgive as you are faithful to keep all of your promises. May nothing deter him from being faithfully devoted to you. And may I be a living example of faithfulness to you. In Jesus' name, amen.

Remember: God is faithful to keep all of his promises.

One Who
Encourages Others

Therefore encourage (admonish, exhort) one another and edify
(strengthen and build up) one another. (1 Thessalonians 5:11 AMP)

Praise God: For he is the Word of Life.

Confess: Any selfishness that blinds me to the needs of others
and keeps me from being an encourager.

Offer Thanks: That our loving God wants us to encourage and
be encouraged in life as we minister his Word to one another.

Ask God: Heavenly Father, Word of Life, may my child
encourage, exhort, edify, strengthen, and build up others.
Instead of seeking to be encouraged, may he look for opportunities to be an encourager. Cultivate in him a desire to come
alongside others — family members, friends, and even people
he may not know — to give an encouraging word. May each
day heighten his awareness of opportunities to edify others
or to give the encouragement of a helping hand. I ask that he
would experience the joy of seeing the people he has helped
gain strength and hope simply because he took the time to
put their needs ahead of his own. Lord, may he spend time
in your Word daily to receive your encouragement and be
strengthened in his faith so that he can build others up. In
Jesus' name, amen.

Remember: God is our comforter and great encourager.

For God's Care
during a Time of Suffering

[The Lord] has not despised or disdained the suffering of the afflicted one; he has not hidden his face from him but has listened to his cry for help. (Psalm 22:24)

Praise God: That he is our Father who cares.

Confess: Any lack of caring for those who need help in the midst of their suffering.

Offer Thanks: That God hears my cries for help and does not turn away from me when I suffer.

Ask God: O caring Father, I am grateful that you have not despised or disdained the suffering of my afflicted child. I thank you that you have not hidden your face from her but have listened to her cry for help. May she sense your presence and care during this time when so many of her friends seem to have forgotten her. She is struggling to deal with the difficult challenges she faces, and the feeling of being abandoned and unloved adds to her pain. Help her trust you moment by moment in the midst of her suffering. I pray that you would relieve her suffering, but if in your wisdom, you allow it to continue, may she find your grace sufficient and discover that your power is truly made perfect in her weakness. Help me, Father, to be a faithful reflection of your unsurpassed mercy and love for her. In Jesus' name, amen.

Remember: Because of God's great care for us, he does not turn away from us when we suffer.

A Plea for a Child
Who Has Gone Astray

I will give them an undivided heart and put a new spirit in them;
I will remove from them their heart of stone and give them a heart
of flesh. (Ezekiel 11:19)

Praise God: Who is our Good Shepherd.

Confess: Any doubt that God will work a miracle in my child's heart.

Offer Thanks: That God, the faithful Shepherd, is watching over my child, even though he has gone astray.

Ask God: O blessed Good Shepherd, I pray that you would give my child an undivided heart and put a new spirit in him. Remove from him his heart of stone and give him a heart of flesh. I plead for his life. He is one of your precious lambs who has gone astray. The ways of the world have led him into behaviors that are destroying his soul. Turn his stubborn, self-willed heart into a heart that is pliable and responsive to your Spirit. Help him come to his senses and see your great love for him regardless of the path he has taken. May your loving-kindness cause him to repent and surrender his whole life to you. You have begun a good work in him, and I trust your promise to carry it to completion until Christ returns. Lord, as I pour out my broken heart to you, may today be the day he turns his heart toward home. In Jesus' name, amen.

Remember: God is the Good Shepherd who seeks out and saves those who are lost.

Guarding against Temptation

Keep alert and pray. Otherwise temptation will overpower you.
For though the spirit is willing enough, the body is weak!
(Matthew 26:41 NLT 1996)

Praise God: Who is our Rock.

Confess: Any lack of diligence in guarding against temptation.

Offer Thanks: To God, who keeps us anchored to the Rock of our salvation.

Ask God: O blessed Rock, I pray that my child will keep alert and pray. Otherwise temptation will overpower him. For though his spirit is willing enough, his body is weak. So please give him spiritual insight to see clearly the dangerous enticements offered by the world, the flesh, and the Devil. Keep my son in a state of watchfulness as he stays close to you, reads the Word daily, prays, and associates with strong believers. When temptation comes, may he turn to you, the Rock of his salvation. May he immediately pray for your help and not trust his own strength. By the power of your Spirit, enable him to say no. I ask you to bring someone to him at his very moment of weakness to help him make the right decision. Give him victory for your glory. In Jesus' name, amen.

Remember: God is our Rock, that we might stand firm in his will.

Diligent in Guarding One's Heart

Watch over your heart with all diligence, for from it flow the springs of life. (Proverbs 4:23 NASB)

Praise God: Who is our teacher.

Confess: Any carelessness or indifference about what I take into my heart.

Offer Thanks: To God, who teaches us to guard our hearts so that we may have full, abundant lives.

Ask God: O faithful Teacher, I pray that my child will watch over his heart with all diligence, for from it flow the springs of life. Father, I am grateful that you are faithful to enable him to do what you command. May my child not be careless or indifferent about what he allows to enter his heart, for it is the "control center" of his intellect, emotions, and will. May he not allow his eyes to watch worthless things. May he be discerning about what he listens to that could turn him away from you. Help him to guard his heart like a sacred treasure, not allowing any defilement to tarnish it. May he be purposeful in choosing you above all else and intentional about filling his heart with the truth of your Word. Keep him watchful through unceasing prayer so that he does not enter into temptation. In Jesus' name, amen.

Remember: God is a faithful teacher, helping us walk in righteousness.

Resist Temptation
by Watching and Praying

Watch *and* pray so that you will not fall into temptation. The spirit
is willing, but the body is weak. (Matthew 26:41)

Praise God: Who is our Intercessor.

Confess: Any personal weaknesses or blind spots that open
the door to temptation.

Offer Thanks: That God gives us his strength to resist
temptation.

Ask God: O blessed Intercessor, I pray that my child will watch
and pray so that he will not fall into temptation. The spirit is
willing, but the body is weak. Give him a heart that is on the
lookout for anything that would tempt him to commit sin.
May he humble himself, recognizing the truth that he cannot in his own flesh keep from succumbing to temptation.
He needs the filling of your Spirit to keep him from making
wrong decisions. Give him the desire to choose you over his
fleshly passions and to go to you in prayer for help to keep him
on the righteous path. To know right and not do it is sin, so I
ask you to help him watch and pray so that he will do what is
right. In Jesus' name, amen.

Remember: God our Intercessor helps us in our weakness.

Trusting and Obeying God's Commands for Marriage

Do not be yoked together with unbelievers. For what do righteousness and wickedness have in common? Or what fellowship can light have with darkness? (2 Corinthians 6:14)

Praise God: Who is our righteous Father.

Confess: Any desire to join together what God says cannot be joined.

Offer Thanks: That God cares about our most intimate and important relationships.

Ask God: O righteous Father, I pray that my child will not be yoked together with unbelievers but will ask, what do righteousness and wickedness have in common? Or what fellowship can light have with darkness? Father, it is never too early for me to pray for my son's choice of a marriage partner. I pray that he will not listen to the lies of the Enemy but instead will wait on you for a spouse who loves you with all her heart, soul, mind, and strength, and who will love her neighbor as herself. Help him see that much heartache and pain will result if he ignores your command and goes his own way. Most high God, Captain of the heavenly hosts, send ministering angels to guard and guide his steps in this most important decision. Bless him with a bride of your choosing, that they might serve you together and raise godly children for your glory. In Jesus' name, amen.

Remember: God is our holy, trustworthy Father, who desires what is best for us.

Turn Away from Lust

I made a covenant with my eyes not to look with lust upon a young woman. (Job 31:1 NLT 1996)

Praise God: Exalt God's holiness.

Confess: Any tendency to look at others with lust rather than with the respect and purity God desires.

Offer Thanks: That God desires every person he has created to be respected, honored, and protected.

Ask God: Sovereign, holy Lord, I pray that my child would make a covenant with his eyes not to look with lust upon a young woman. May he agree with you not to look with lust at women whom you lovingly created in your image. Empower him by your Holy Spirit not to give in to the darkness of his lustful passions. Turn his heart toward Jesus, not his selfish, fleshly desires. May he keep his mind steadfast in purity by renewing his mind in your Word each day. May he stand firm in all the will of God. Preserve his life in your righteousness. For your glory, may he be found faithful, in Jesus' name, amen.

Remember: God is holy, pure in all his ways.

Deliverance from Pornography

Some sat in darkness and the deepest gloom, prisoners suffering in iron chains, for they had rebelled against the words of God and despised the counsel of the Most High.... Then they cried to the LORD in their trouble, and he saved them from their distress. He brought them out of darkness and the deepest gloom and broke away their chains. (Psalm 107:10, 11, 13, 14)

Praise God: Who is our deliverer.

Confess: Any inclination to walk toward darkness rather than in the light of God's ways.

Offer Thanks: For God's deliverance and mighty power to save.

Ask God: My great Deliverer, I cry out in desperation for my child. He is sitting in darkness and deepest gloom, a prisoner suffering in iron chains, for he has rebelled against your words and despised the counsel of the Most High. As he cries out to you in his trouble, save him from his distress. Bring him out of darkness and deepest gloom. Break away his chains. O Lord, my son is caught in the web of pornography. Save him from this evil. Break this stronghold. Lift him out of the miry pit and set his feet on the Rock of Jesus. Holy Spirit, I ask that your conviction would fall heavily on his heart so that he sees his sin as you see it. Lead him to godly sorrow and repentance. And when he has turned back to you, may he be a light to others caught in this dark web, for your name's sake. In Jesus' name, amen.

Remember: God is our Redeemer, who delivers us from the darkness of sin.

Repentance Leads to Restoration

This is what the LORD says: "If you repent, I will restore you that you may serve me." (Jeremiah 15:19)

Praise God: For he restores.

Confess: Any doubt that God is faithful to forgive and restore me when I repent.

Offer Thanks: That when God forgives, he remembers my sin no more.

Ask God: O blessed Father who restores, comfort my child with your promise that if he repents, you will restore him that he may serve you. Father, you know he has sincerely repented. By your grace may he believe that you forgave him immediately and fully. Please help him now to forgive himself, and I ask you to restore the joy of his salvation. Remove his fear that he can't serve you in the work of your kingdom because of his past sin. Give him faith to believe that you will work even this for good, for your glory and the furtherance of your kingdom. In Jesus' name, amen.

Remember: Our merciful God forgives completely and restores fully.

Having Confidence
in the Strength of Christ

I have strength for all things in Christ Who empowers me — [I am ready for anything and equal to anything through Him Who infuses inner strength into me; I am self-sufficient in Christ's sufficiency]. (Philippians 4:13 AMP)

Praise God: Who is all-sufficient.

Confess: Any lack of dependence on Christ's sufficiency.

Offer Thanks: To God, who strengthens us for and in all things.

Ask God: All-sufficient God, I ask you to give my child confidence that she has strength for all things in Christ who empowers her. She is ready for anything and equal to anything through you who infuses her with inner strength. She is self-sufficient in Christ's sufficiency. May she boldly tackle each difficult task with the confident assurance that you are sufficient to equip her to complete the job well. May she not boast or be arrogant when she succeeds but be quick to give you the glory for her accomplishments. May she not live in fear, self-doubt, or insecurity but be confident because her all-sufficient Father provides all she needs. In Jesus' name, amen.

Remember: God is our strength, power, and hope.

God's Passionate Desire
for Personal Relationship

You must worship no other gods, but only the LORD, for he is a
God who is passionate about his relationship with you.
(Exodus 34:14 NLT 1996)

Praise God: For his passionate love.

Confess: Any lack of desire or commitment for a deep relationship with God.

Offer Thanks: That almighty God, our Father, desires to have a personal relationship with each of us.

Ask God: O passionate, loving Father, I pray that my child will not worship any other gods, but only you, for you are a God who is passionate about your relationship with her. Give her a longing to develop a strong, loving, warm, close friendship with you. May you be her number-one companion. May she come to you often because she has an insatiable desire to hear your voice, to know your heart, and to walk in your ways. Help her know that she can share anything with you: her joys, sorrows, cares, and concerns. May she feel highly valued knowing that you passionately desire a relationship with her. May her loving intimacy with you eliminate any temptation to pursue other gods. In Jesus' name, amen.

Remember: God longs to be our personal Father, friend, and companion.

Emotions That Affect Physical Health

A calm and undisturbed mind and heart are the life and health of the body, but envy, jealousy, and wrath are like rottenness of the bones. (Proverbs 14:30 AMP)

Praise God: Who is our protector.

Confess: Any indulgence in destructive emotions, such as envy, jealousy, or wrath.

Offer Thanks: To God, who warns us against the personal harm of walking in darkness.

Ask God: O God who protects, I ask that my child would have a calm, undisturbed mind and heart, which are the life and health of his body. I pray that he will not allow envy, jealousy, and wrath to dwell in his heart, for they are like rottenness to his bones. I pray for him to have a healthy mind filled with the wisdom and knowledge of you. May he be careful to not entertain thoughts of envy or wanting what others have. I ask that he would diligently guard his mind against being jealous of others because of their appearance, possessions, or talents. Show him that indulgence in these emotions leads only to a complaining, discontented, and joyless life. I pray for a grateful, contented heart and a tranquil, peaceful mind for my son. Keep anger and resentment far from him so that he will live a healthy life in body and spirit. In Jesus' name, amen.

Remember: God is our protector — the giver of life, peace, and health.

Accepting Constructive Criticism

Let the righteous smite me in kindness and reprove me; it is oil upon the head; do not let my head refuse it. (Psalm 141:5 NASB)

Praise God: For his loving-kindness.

Confess: Any resentment or rejection of a kind reproof.

Offer Thanks: For God's kind reproof that leads us to righteousness.

Ask God: O most loving, kind Lord, let the righteous smite my child in kindness and reprove him. It is oil on his head. May he not refuse it but learn from it. May he take seriously the kind, constructive criticism that comes to him. May he show respect for the one who confronts him. Help him listen with a receptive heart, not trying to justify, blame, or make excuses for himself. If his offenses need forgiveness, I ask that he would humble himself and repent. May he recognize reproof as a spiritual blessing motivated by your great love, and may he accept it with gladness. In Jesus' name, amen.

Remember: In his loving-kindness, God leads us in righteousness.

To Be a Person Who Speaks Truth

So put away all falsehood and "tell your neighbor the truth."
(Ephesians 4:25 NLT 1996)

Praise God: That he is truth.

Confess: Any false dealings in my relationships with others.

Offer Thanks: That we can trust our loving God to always be truthful with us.

Ask God: God of all truth, I implore you to help my child put away all falsehood and tell others the truth. Lord, if she is guilty of a lie, may she be caught and not get away with it. When she is confronted about a lie, may she be humble and have a repentant heart. May she immediately ask forgiveness from you and others. When she is tempted to lie, please empower her by your Holy Spirit to speak truth and reflect your likeness. I ask that she would find the joy of a clean conscience and restored fellowship to be worth the price of telling the truth. May she be known as a person who can be trusted because she speaks the truth with a sincere heart. In the name of Jesus, amen.

Remember: God is true in all of his relationships and wants us to walk in his truth.

Hope for Depression

Why are you downcast, O my soul? Why so disturbed within me?
Put your hope in God, for I will yet praise him, my Savior and my
God. (Psalm 42:11)

Praise God: That he is the God of all hope.

Confess: Any doubt of God's love and care for me.

Offer Thanks: That God saves us from all evil and gives us
hope for life on earth and in eternity.

Ask God: God of all hope, I cry out for my child who suffers
from depression. Her soul is downcast and disturbed within
her. I pray that she will put her hope in you. May she yet praise
you, her Savior and her God. Father, it breaks my heart and
frightens me to see her in such a dark place. Every day is a
struggle. She feels so hopeless and wants so much to be whole
and healthy. Give her endurance to press on. Grant her faith
to believe that your plans for her are good. By your grace may
she feel your love. I ask for your mercy to heal my daughter
and to give her a heart of hope. Give me wisdom to know how
to help her, and grant me strength and courage to do it. You
promise that if we hope in you, we will not be disappointed.
Keep us looking to you for hope. In Jesus' name, amen.

Remember: God is our Savior and our hope.

Living with
Mental Illness

Cast all your anxiety on him because he cares for you. (1 Peter 5:7)

Praise God: Who cares.

Confess: The times when anxiety and fear cause me to forget that God cares for me.

Offer Thanks: That my caring God reminds me to give my burdens to him so that I can receive his peace.

Ask God: My blessed, caring God, I pray that my child will cast all his anxiety on you because you care for him. Father, you know the difficulty we have had in diagnosing and treating his mental illness. I cry out to you to heal my son and give him a sound mind. Please lead us to the right doctors. Give them wisdom to find the best course of treatment. Father, you see the torment my son suffers daily. You know how fearful and agitated he becomes. Even during those most difficult moments, I pray that you will make known to him the wonderful truth that you personally love him, care deeply for him, and never create anything that is a mistake. Please answer his spoken and unspoken cries for help. Give him assurance that you hear him. May I be sensitive to times when I can offer hope by sharing your promises with him. When I am overwrought with anxiety, help me cast my cares on you and trust that your perfect will and purposes will be done in my son's life. In Jesus' name, amen.

Remember: God cares deeply for us in our suffering.

Release from
the Shame of Abuse

But You, O Lord, are a shield for me, my glory, and the lifter of my head. (Psalm 3:3 AMP)

Praise God: Who is our shield.

Confess: The times I become engrossed in shame and guilt, losing sight of my Savior's forgiveness at the cross.

Offer Thanks: To God, who shields us by the power of his glorious love so that we can walk in confidence.

Ask God: O Lord my shield, I pray that you will be a shield for my daughter. Be her glory and the lifter of her head. Protect her from falling into dark thoughts of shame because of the abuse she has suffered. Remind her again that what happened was not her fault. Lift her head above those painful memories. Show her your glory over and over by transforming her shame into redemption so that she can lift her head as an overcomer. By the power of your redeeming love, may she know and celebrate her purity as your beloved daughter. In Jesus' name, amen.

Remember: No matter what shameful memories we carry, God is our shield of protection and desires to lift us up.

Endurance for Prolonged Sickness

The LORD will sustain him on his sickbed and restore him from his bed of illness. (Psalm 41:3)

Praise God: Who sustains.

Confess: Any doubt of God's loving care or power to heal when I suffer from illness.

Offer Thanks: That God watches over us and sustains us when we are sick.

Ask God: God who sustains, I ask that you will sustain my child on his sickbed. Please restore him from his bed of illness. Jesus, throughout your ministry on earth, you proved yourself to be God through healing. You are the all-powerful God, and nothing is too hard for you. I trust that you will restore my child to health and strength. He is suffering from a long and difficult illness. He is weak and weary of the struggle. Please give him strength and courage to bear up under his illness. May he feel a special sense of your nearness and your great love for him that eliminates his fears. I thank you for your love and healing grace. In Jesus' name, amen.

Remember: God, who mercifully and lovingly sustains us.

Being Afraid to Sleep
or Unable to Sleep

I will lie down in peace and sleep, for you alone, O LORD, will keep me safe. (Psalm 4:8 NLT 1996)

Praise God: Who is our protector.

Confess: Any times I have doubted God's watchful, protective care.

Offer Thanks: That God our protector is mighty in power and gentle in spirit, taking my child's mind from fear to faith.

Ask God: Almighty Protector, may my child lie down in peace and sleep, for you alone, O Lord, will keep her safe. Please give her the calm assurance that she has nothing to fear because you are with her and have the power to keep her safe during the night. I ask you to send ministering angels to calm her heart and body so that she can fall asleep and wake up refreshed in the morning. May your Word comfort her and bring peace to her heart before she goes to bed. Grant me strength, loving patience, and creative ideas to help her through this season of fear. In Jesus' name, amen.

Remember: God is our protector, who offers safety, peace, and rest to his children.

Be Courageous! God Never Leaves Those Who Belong to Him

Be strong and courageous. Do not be afraid or terrified ... for the LORD your God goes with you; he will never leave you nor forsake you. (Deuteronomy 31:6)

Praise God: The Chief Shepherd.

Confess: Any lack of confidence in God's presence with me.

Offer Thanks: That God our Shepherd goes with us, giving strength and courage to face whatever lies ahead.

Ask God: O Lord my Shepherd, I ask that my child would be strong and courageous. May he not be afraid or terrified, for you, Lord, go with him. May he always know that you will never leave him or forsake him. I pray that he would stand firmly and fearlessly in the truth that you sealed his salvation by your Holy Spirit when he asked you into his heart. Give him assurance that no matter where he is, you are right there with him and will be with him all the way to heaven. May he know that if he needs help, you are there. If he needs courage, you are there. If he needs self-control, you are there. If he needs forgiveness, you are there. May he be confident in every situation because you are there. In Jesus' name, amen.

Remember: God, our Chief Shepherd, never leaves us alone.

A Plea for a Healing Miracle

As Jesus approached Jericho, a blind man was sitting by the road-side begging.... He called out, "Jesus, Son of David, have mercy on me!" ... Jesus asked him, "What do you want me to do for you?" "Lord, I want to see," he replied. Jesus said to him, "Receive your sight; your faith has healed you." Immediately he received his sight and followed Jesus, praising God. (Luke 18:35, 38, 40–43)

Praise God: Who is our healer.

Confess: Any doubt of God's power to do what is impossible for me.

Offer Thanks: That God is powerful enough to perform miracles.

Ask God: Almighty God who heals, when Jesus asked the blind man begging by the roadside, "What do you want me to do for you?" the man said, "I want to see." And you healed him. Father, in the same way, I cry out for your mercy on my child. Just as the blind man could not find healing from the physicians of his day, my daughter's physicians offer her no cure. So I boldly come before you with my petition: I want you to heal my daughter for your glory. May her health be restored so that she may follow you, praising your name. You are the same yesterday, today, and forever, and I believe you are able to heal, if it be in your plan and your will. In Jesus' name, amen.

Remember: Nothing is too hard for our God, who is able to heal.

Trusting God to Be Faithful

This I recall to my mind, therefore I have hope. The LORD's lovingkindnesses indeed never cease, for His compassions never fail. They are new every morning; great is Your faithfulness. (Lamentations 3:21–23 NASB)

Praise God: Who is great in faithfulness.

Confess: The times I lose hope because I do not trust God's faithfulness.

Offer Thanks: By recalling how God has been faithful to me every day.

Ask God: O faithful Father, I ask that my child would recall this to her mind and therefore have hope: The Lord's loving-kindnesses indeed never cease, for his compassions never fail. They are new every morning; great is your faithfulness. Father, my daughter is experiencing difficult, troubling times. I ask that you would cause her to keep her eyes on you and remember your promise that your compassions are new each day. May she experience your peace, trusting that no matter where life takes her, your mercies are more than adequate to meet her every need. Please give her strength when she is weak, wisdom when she is confused, and encouragement when she is fearful. With a heart of hope, I look forward to seeing your mercies and compassions unfold in her life. In Jesus' name, amen.

Remember: God is faithful; his promises are sure.

Remain Fully Committed to God

The eyes of the LORD range throughout the earth to strengthen those whose hearts are fully committed to him. (2 Chronicles 16:9)

Praise God: Who is all-knowing.

Confess: The times I think my walk with God is all on my shoulders and feel too weak or weary to fulfill my commitment to him.

Offer Thanks: That God gives me all the strength I need to do whatever he asks of me.

Ask God: Omniscient, all-knowing Father, may my child be comforted knowing that as your eyes range throughout the earth, you will strengthen his heart because he is fully committed to you. Lord, work in my son's heart that he might be found faithful, serving you with pure motives. May he live in the confident assurance that you will provide all the strength he needs — body, soul, mind, and spirit — to fulfill what he has committed to you. During difficult, lonely, and painful times, I ask you to strengthen him with your glorious might so that he will press on, resolved to be fully committed to you no matter what. May he daily commit himself to serve the Savior he loves. In Jesus' name, amen.

Remember: Our all-knowing God watches over and strengthens those who are fully committed to him.

Safe in the Name of the Lord

The name of the LORD is a strong tower; the righteous run to it and are safe. (Proverbs 18:10)

Praise God: For being a strong tower.

Confess: Any times I have not treasured and honored the powerful name of the Lord.

Offer Thanks: That the powerful name of the Lord safely embraces us, protecting us from all harm.

Ask God: O God, my strong tower, I pray for my child to trust that your name is her strong tower; as your righteous child, she can run to it and be safe. Lord, she needs your protection. She is feeling spiritually threatened, almost as if she is being stalked by a dark presence that seeks to harm her. I pray that during these times of fear, panic, worry, and confusion, her immediate reaction will be to call on your powerful name for help. May her first instinct be to run — not walk — to your strong tower of safety, where all your names, attributes, and characteristics dwell. May she find sweet solace in trusting her God, who is able to keep her safe and protect her from all the threats of the Enemy. Lord, manifest your nature to my daughter in her time of need, providing strength for the journey, peace for her heart, ointment for her wounds, and rest for her weary soul. May she proclaim that it is good to be near God, for she has made you, sovereign Lord, her refuge. In Jesus' name, amen.

Remember: The mighty power of the Lord's name will never fail.

Strengthened
by the Belt of Truth

Stand firm then, with the belt of truth buckled around your waist.
(Ephesians 6:14)

Praise God: Who never changes.

Confess: Any wavering of my faith concerning the truth of God's Word and my salvation through Christ.

Offer Thanks: For the powerful, never-changing truth that Jesus is the way, the truth, and the life.

Ask God: Immutable God who never changes, I ask that my child would stand firm, with the belt of truth buckled around his waist. Whenever he is discouraged, defeated, depressed, or feeling helpless, may he remember that Jesus is the way, the truth, and the life. Give him unwavering faith during those times of weakness to remember that Jesus — who came to earth to save sinners by dying and rising from the dead and thereby gaining the victory over Satan — lives in his heart. Grant him the assurance that because of the power of Christ in his life, he is ready to fight whatever the Enemy dishes out. In the thick of battle, arm him with the belt of your truth. May he grow in spiritual insight to see that Jesus shows himself as truth through the power of his Word. In Jesus' name, amen.

Remember: God never changes: He is the way, the truth, and the life.

Stand Strong in the Righteousness of God

Stand firm then ... with the breastplate of righteousness in place.
(Ephesians 6:14)

Praise God: For he is our righteousness.

Confess: Any false confidence or pride I may have in my self-righteousness.

Offer Thanks: That Jesus came down from heaven and gave himself to be my righteousness.

Ask God: O blessed, righteous Lord, I cry out for my child to stand firm with the breastplate of righteousness in place. I pray that she will know beyond a shadow of a doubt that she received the breastplate of righteousness the moment she accepted Christ as her Lord and Savior. Father, when she struggles with her failures and shortcomings as a Christian, please guard her heart from the Enemy's lies that you don't love her and won't forgive her sins. Plant the truth in her heart that through Jesus' victory on the cross, she has been made holy in your sight. Give her the blessed assurance that Jesus is her righteousness and that she is a daughter of the King. May she answer the Enemy's attacks by remembering that she wears the breastplate of righteousness and stands not on her own merit but on the merit of Christ her Lord. May she walk righteously in all your ways. In Jesus' name, amen.

Remember: God is our righteousness, and no power can stand against him.

Stand Firm in Peace

Stand firm then ... with your feet fitted with the readiness that
comes from the gospel of peace. (Ephesians 6:14–15)

Praise God: Who is the Prince of Peace.

Confess: The times I allow the fears of the moment to rob
me of peace.

Offer Thanks: That God, the Prince of Peace, gives me peace
that passes all understanding.

Ask God: Prince of Peace, I pray that my child would stand
firm, with his feet fitted with the readiness that comes from
the gospel of peace. May he know that by accepting Christ,
he has peace with his heavenly Father. Settle this truth in
his heart: whatever he faces, you are the warrior at his right
hand who is ready to give him strength, courage, hope, and
protection in the battle. Keep his feet firmly planted on the
truth of your Word and of who you are. When he is anxious
and fearful, help him cast his every care on you so that he
might experience your peace that passes all understanding. O
Father, there is no greater joy than to know that my son has
made peace with you. Now please guard his heart and mind
and guide his feet to others he can tell about the eternal peace
found in your Son, Jesus Christ. In Jesus' name, amen.

Remember: God is the Prince of Peace, who offers eternal
peace to us.

Take Up
the Shield of Faith

Take up the shield of faith, with which you can extinguish all the
flaming arrows of the evil one. (Ephesians 6:16)

Praise God: Who is our shield of faith.

Confess: Any hesitation in using the shield of faith against
Satan's attacks.

Offer Thanks: That God has given me his incredible shield of
faith to protect my heart from the Enemy's lies.

Ask God: O God my shield, I ask that my child would take up
your shield of faith, with which he can extinguish all the flaming arrows of the Evil One. When Satan's arrows fly toward
him at rapid speed, strengthen him to take up your shield
so that he can defeat any attack. Help him understand that
the Enemy's arrows are very real, assaulting his character and
faith. In the midst of the battles he faces, may he learn not to
rely on himself but to trust wholeheartedly in you to protect
him from the lies and temptations Satan hurls at him. May my
son always be ready to take up your shield and boldly declare
his trust in you. I pray that as he uses this powerful weapon,
he will grow in unwavering faith. In the mighty name of Jesus,
amen.

Remember: God is our shield and protects us from Satan's
flaming arrows as we declare our faith in him.

Put On the
Helmet of Salvation

Put on salvation as your helmet. (Ephesians 6:17 NLT 1996)

Praise God: Who is our Savior.

Confess: The times I allow wrong thinking instead of taking my thoughts captive to the obedience of Christ.

Offer Thanks: That Christ's saving work on the cross sets me free from the Enemy's enslavement to wrong thinking.

Ask God: O Lord my Savior, I ask that my child would put on the helmet of salvation to protect herself in the spiritual battle for her mind. Fix deeply in her mind the truth of her salvation. When Satan attacks her mind with doubts, fears, and accusations, help her remember that she is in Christ, and Christ is in her. By your grace, give her an unquenchable desire to daily renew her mind by the transforming power of your Word, and take every thought captive to the obedience of Christ so that she will not be disarmed by the chaos around her. I pray that you will protect her from wrong thoughts, confused thinking, and every evil that is vying for her mind. May she daily submit her mind, will, and emotions to the authority of your Spirit until the day of Jesus' return. In Jesus' name, amen.

Remember: Our God and Savior has given us his Word to renew our minds.

Our Weapon for Battle: The Sword of the Spirit

Take ... the sword of the Spirit, which is the word of God.
(Ephesians 6:17)

Praise God: Who is the Word.

Confess: The times I waver in my faith because I am not fully trusting the Word of God.

Offer Thanks: That God protects us from all evil by the mighty power of his Word.

Ask God: O mighty Word, I pray that my child will take hold of the sword of the Spirit, which is the Word of God. May he have confidence that your Word is both an offensive and defensive spiritual weapon that is infinitely more powerful than any of Satan's weapons. Help him wield your Word by faith in the name of Jesus. May your powerful, effective, and instructive Word dwell in him richly, making him strong for the very real battles he will encounter every day. I plead for my son that he would be a man of the Word who proclaims and defends the truth. Protect him from anything that would keep him from reading and obeying your Word. May your words be more precious than gold to him, and may he meditate on your Word day and night so that he will be equipped to do battle for the kingdom of God. In Jesus' name, amen.

Remember: God is the Word, who arms us for battle.

To Grow in Self-Control

But the fruit of the Spirit is ... self-control.
(Galatians 5:22–23 NASB)

Praise God: For he is patient.

Confess: Any tendency to spiral out of control in word or action.

Offer Thanks: That God sent his Spirit to help us learn to walk in godliness.

Ask God: Patient Father, I ask that my child would be led by the Holy Spirit to exhibit the fruit of self-control in his life. Grant him the self-discipline he so desperately needs to restrain himself. O Lord, by the power of your Holy Spirit, give him the presence of mind to stop himself when he is tempted to indulge his emotions or appetites. Keep him from spiraling out of control, and help him listen with understanding to sound reasoning. May he recognize his out-of-control actions as sin and ask for forgiveness. Give him faith to believe that when he asks for your help, he can expect to receive it. Lord, I need your wisdom to know how to partner with your Spirit in teaching and modeling how to grow in self-control. In Jesus' name, amen.

Remember: God is patient, good, and kind in all of his dealings with us.

To Live in Integrity

Rid yourselves of all malice and all deceit. (1 Peter 2:1)

Praise God: Who is pure.

Confess: Any desire to deceive or any thoughts of ill will toward others.

Offer Thanks: That God is honest and faithful, never wanting to bring harm to us.

Ask God: O blessed, pure God, I pray that my child will rid himself of all malice and all deceit. May she be pure in motive and trustworthy in action, not misleading others by making a false impression or leading them to believe something that isn't true. Protect her from the desire to cause physical, verbal, or emotional harm to others. May she not be deceitful and try to cover up her lies or wrongdoing. Please, Lord, if she ever steps on that slippery slope of deceitfulness, may she get caught, no matter how painful it is, and may she respond with true repentance, grieving over her sin. Father, I pray that she will recognize every time she is prone to be deceptive or malicious and will choose instead to walk in paths of righteousness, honoring you and obeying your commands. In Jesus' name, amen.

Remember: God is trustworthy and true in every way.

Speaking Gracious Words

Do not let any unwholesome talk come out of your mouths,
but only what is helpful for building others up according to their
needs, that it may benefit those who listen. (Ephesians 4:29)

Praise God: That he is gracious.

Confess: Any habits of unwholesome talk that do not benefit
those who hear them.

Offer Thanks: To God, whose words of grace and truth call us
into relationship with him.

Ask God: Gracious Lord, I pray that my child will not let any
unwholesome talk come out of her mouth, but only what is
helpful for building others up according to their needs, that
it may benefit those who listen. I pray that she will see the
wisdom of learning to hold her tongue and will guard her
mouth to keep herself from calamity. Grant her a kind heart
that speaks edifying words to build up others. Open her spiritual eyes to see how reckless words can pierce the heart. Help
her to stop and think before she speaks, so she doesn't say
something that would wound others. May people be amazed
by the gracious words that come from her lips, just like the
gracious words of Jesus. I pray this in Jesus' name, amen.

Remember: God's words are gracious, leading us to walk in
his righteousness.

Sharing God's Light through Good Deeds

Let your light shine before men, that they may see your good deeds and praise your Father in heaven. (Matthew 5:16)

Praise God: Who is the Light of the World.

Confess: Any attitudes or actions that darken the light of God within me.

Offer Thanks: That God has shown us the light of his salvation.

Ask God: Dear God of light, may my child let her light shine before others, that they may see her good deeds and praise her Father in heaven. I ask that her good deeds would be a witness pointing others to the Christ who lives in her. Grant her a pure heart in her acts of service, not a heart that seeks recognition or admiration. May she not be compelled to serve because she feels pressure from others to perform. Give her the joy of knowing that even if no one else knows about her good deeds, you do, and you are her reward. Continue to grow in her a heart of service to others in love, for the glory of God. In Jesus' name, amen.

Remember: God is light, and there is no darkness in him.

Known for a Gentle Spirit

Let your gentleness be evident to all. (Philippians 4:5)

Praise God: For he is gentle.

Confess: Any tendency to be harsh, impatient, or demanding of others.

Offer Thanks: That God made his gentleness evident to me.

Ask God: O gentle Jesus, I pray that my child's gentleness would be evident to all. Reveal to him that a gentle spirit is a humble spirit. Develop in him a heart that is gentle, compassionate, and merciful toward the needs, faults, and failures of others. May he be gracious and patient in every encounter. Help him exhibit self-control so that he will not be quick to retaliate, speak harshly, intimidate, or bark out demands. May his soothing and calm conversation be attractive to others and point them to the gentle Jesus who lives in him. Thank you, Jesus, for showing your gentleness to us. May your gentleness be evident in my heart and life as well. In your name I pray, amen.

Remember: God is gentle, kind, and forgiving.

Freedom from
a Judgmental Spirit

Do not judge, or you too will be judged. For in the same way you judge others, you will be judged, and with the measure you use, it will be measured to you. (Matthew 7:1–2)

Praise God: For he is just.

Confess: Any tendency toward hasty, harsh, or unkind judgments against others.

Offer Thanks: That God is kind, merciful, and forgiving in his justice.

Ask God: O divine, just God, I pray that my child will not judge, because he too will be judged. For in the same way he judges others, he will be judged, and with the measure he uses, it will be measured to him. Lord, I ask that you would reveal to him when he has a critical spirit that leads to quick, negative judgments of others without knowing all the facts. Help him see that judgments he thinks are fair are really judgments flowing from a heart rooted in self-righteousness, hurt, or bitterness. Convict him of his condemning accusations. Free him of blaming and passing sentence on others. Grant him humility that he might forgive and be set free. May his life demonstrate the same mercy and forgiveness that you have shown by the debt you paid for him. In Jesus' name, amen.

Remember: God is just and loving, quick to forgive all our offenses.

Choosing Words
God Would Use

Be imitators of God, therefore.... There must not be ... obscenity, foolish talk or coarse joking, which are out of place, but rather thanksgiving. (Ephesians 5:1, 3, 4)

Praise God: Who sanctifies.

Confess: Any times I indulge in filthy talk, cursing, foolish talk, or coarse joking.

Offer Thanks: That God offers himself as a faithful example of the words and thoughts that are acceptable in his sight.

Ask God: Dear Lord who sanctifies, I ask that my child would be an imitator of you. May no obscenity, foolish talk, or coarse joking, which are out of place, flow from her mouth, but rather thanksgiving. Protect her mind from the ungodly language of cussing and swearing that she hears at school, in the workplace, and on television and other media. May she not take part in filthy jokes, sexual slurs, or nasty gossip that would hurt the feelings or harm the reputation of another person. Help her understand that foul, abusive language is never acceptable. May she desire that the words of her mouth and the meditations of her heart would be acceptable in your sight. Instead of cursing, may blessings of thanksgiving pour forth from her mouth. In Jesus' name, amen.

Remember: The Lord our God sacrificed himself for our salvation and sanctifies us for his glory.

Living by the Golden Rule

Do for others what you would like them to do for you.
(Matthew 7:12 NLT 1996)

Praise God: Who is kind.

Confess: Any acts of selfishness in my relationships with others.

Offer Thanks: For how kind and generous God is.

Ask God: O kindhearted God, I ask that my child would do for others what he would like them to do for him. I pray that he would treat others as he would like to be treated. In situations where he wants to push to the front, dominate the conversation, be bossy, or take the biggest and the best for himself, may he pause to consider the needs of others. Give him an unselfish heart that desires to serve others before himself. May he not expect anything in return but enjoy the inner satisfaction of pleasing you. Continue to develop in his character the habit of treating others as he would like to be treated. For your glory and his joy. In Jesus' name, amen.

Remember: God is kind and loving in all of his dealings with us.

Love Your Enemies

Love your enemies, do good to them, and lend to them without
expecting to get anything back. Then your reward will be great,
and you will be sons of the Most High, because he is kind to the
ungrateful and wicked. Be merciful, just as your Father is merciful.
(Luke 6:35–36)

Praise God: For he is merciful.

Confess: Any times I have held back in doing good to those I
think don't deserve it.

Offer Thanks: That God is kind, generous, and merciful to
everyone, even those who are ungrateful and wicked.

Ask God: O merciful Father, I ask that my child would love his
enemies, do good to them, and lend to them without expecting to get anything back. Then his reward will be great, and
he will be a son of the Most High, because you are kind to
the ungrateful and wicked. May my son be merciful, just as
you are merciful. I especially pray that he would show kindness and mercy to the person who has severely wronged him.
Father, when my son is tempted to become vengeful, I ask that
he would turn to prayer instead and choose to love, forgive,
and do good to this person. May my son's kindness convict his
enemy. Bless my child with peace as he obeys your command,
and grant him faith that this will all work together for good
because he chooses to obey you. In Jesus' name, amen.

Remember: God delights in mercy and kindness.

Facing Financial Instability

I have learned the secret of being content in any and every situation, whether well fed or hungry, whether living in plenty or in want. (Philippians 4:12)

Praise God: Who provides.

Confess: My fears and lack of contentment when I face a financial crisis.

Offer Thanks: That God promises to provide what we need.

Ask God: Great Provider, I pray that my child will learn the secret of being content in any and every situation, whether well fed or hungry, whether living in plenty or in want. The financial challenge we face as a family is hard. I pray that you will help my daughter through this transition to a more humble lifestyle. Increase her faith to believe your promise that you will provide for all our needs according to your riches in glory. Give her the desire to do her part to alleviate the financial burden we face. Instead of focusing on what she doesn't have, may she learn to be content and thankful for the good things you have given her. May she learn that no matter what life brings, she can take her needs to you and trust you to provide for her. Help her learn to guard her heart against envy and refuse to indulge in complaining. Help me also to trust you in plenty and in want so that my daughter will see a contented, grateful mom, no matter what my circumstances are. In Jesus' name, amen.

Remember: Our sovereign God provides!

To Work Hard and Not Be Lazy

Work hard and cheerfully at whatever you do, as though you were working for the Lord rather than for people. (Colossians 3:23 NLT 1996)

Praise God: Who is our Lord.

Confess: Any complaining or laziness regarding the work God has given me to do.

Offer Thanks: For the great and mighty works of our Lord's hand.

Ask God: O blessed Lord, I pray that my child will work hard and cheerfully at whatever he does, as though he were working for you rather than for people. Lord, you know my son struggles with being lazy. You have created him with so much potential, and it saddens me that he has a bad attitude. He seems to be disinterested, inactive, slothful, and unmotivated to fulfill his responsibilities at home or school. O Lord, please allow the consequences of his poor choices to be so painful that he seeks your help to change his heart. May he no longer be content with just getting by but seek to possess the qualities of self-discipline, self-control, and diligence in increasing measure so that he will be effective, productive, and joyful in serving you. In Jesus' name, amen.

Remember: Our Lord God works tirelessly on our behalf, providing for our every need.

Keep Your Feet
on the Righteous Path

Make level paths for your feet and take only ways that are firm.
Do not swerve to the right or the left; keep your foot from evil.
(Proverbs 4:26–27)

Praise God: Who is righteous.

Confess: The times my feet swerve to the right or the left, away from God's righteous path.

Offer Thanks: To God for his perfect wisdom and faithfulness in guiding us in the way of righteousness.

Ask God: O Lord my righteousness, I pray that my child will make level paths for his feet and take only ways that are firm. May he not swerve to the right or the left but keep his foot from evil. Father, I pray that you would keep his feet from entering theaters to see movies that would contaminate his heart. Keep his feet from going to parties that would lead him into temptation. Keep his feet far away from dating someone who is not a Christian. Keep his feet from getting into a physical altercation. Keep his feet from sneaking out at night to do foolish things. May he not turn to the right or the left but plant his feet on the firm, unshakable, unchanging foundation of Jesus, who will keep his steps from evil. In Jesus' name, amen.

Remember: God is the way of righteousness, and those who are wise walk with him.

To Be Disciplined
in the Pursuit of Godliness

Discipline yourself for the purpose of godliness.
(1 Timothy 4:7 NASB)

Praise God: Who is holy.

Confess: Any lack of commitment or rigor in my pursuit of godliness.

Offer Thanks: To our holy God, who emptied himself completely so that we can be made pure and holy as he is.

Ask God: O holy God, I ask that my child would discipline herself for the purpose of godliness. Just as an athlete is rigorous and self-sacrificing in training for success, I ask that my child would be committed to training in spiritual disciplines. I pray that she will be faithful in daily reading of the Word and prayer. May her goal each day be to live in your presence and please you in every thought, word, and deed. I pray that she will surround herself with friends who also are disciplined in their desire to grow in godliness. Please bring her mentors to help her keep focused and accountable. Father, please reward her with visible fruit of her labor along the way, especially during those times when she wants to give up. In Jesus' name, amen.

Remember: God is holy, and those who love him seek to be like him.

Eat and Drink for God's Glory

Whether you eat or drink or whatever you do, do it all for the glory of God. (1 Corinthians 10:31)

Praise God: Who is the King of Glory.

Confess: Any indulgence in food or drink or any other habits that show disregard for the work of my King, who cares for me.

Offer Thanks: To God our King, who graciously provides for us so that we might serve him.

Ask God: O blessed King of Glory, I ask that whether my child eats or drinks, or whatever he does, he would do it all for your glory. Please help my child grow in developing an appetite for healthy eating that will benefit him all of his life. Take away his cravings for desserts, sodas, and snacks that leave his body empty of the nutrients it needs and will eventually cause him harm. May his taste buds enjoy foods that will make his body strong and healthy. Lord, I need to put feet to these prayers as well. Help me to be more intentional about planning and making healthy meals. Help me to be a better role model in my own eating habits. Grant me joyful satisfaction in setting the dinner table with appetizing, healthy foods that bring life and health to our bodies rather than death — all for your glory. In Jesus' name, amen.

Remember: God our King created us in his image for his glory.

Learning to Be Gracious, Not Rude

Love … is not rude. (1 Corinthians 13:4, 5 AMP)

Praise God: Who is gracious.

Confess: Any words, attitudes, or behaviors toward others that are quick-tempered, disrespectful, overbearing, or unkind.

Offer Thanks: To my gracious Lord, who is kind, patient, and gentle to me.

Ask God: O most gracious Lord, true love is not rude. Open the eyes of my child's heart to see that selfless love is never rude. Father, you know she struggles with a quick temper. When she doesn't get her way, she raises her voice, broods, and generally behaves badly. O Lord, change her selfish, rude heart into a loving heart that cares about others' feelings and is sensitive to their wishes. Grow in her the ability to be a good listener who doesn't talk over others. May she experience the joy of working together with others without trying to dominate them. Please grant her wisdom to know that what makes her beautiful is a heart like yours that is loving, courteous, polite, and gracious. Grant me wisdom in knowing how to help her grow in these qualities, and help me model them in my behavior as well. In Jesus' name, amen.

Remember: God who loves us is always gracious in his dealings with us.

One Who Loves Refrains from Boasting

Love is not ... boastful. (1 Corinthians 13:4 NLT 1996)

Praise God: That he is supreme.

Confess: Any hint of arrogance or selfishness that leads me to want others to know how worthy of praise I am.

Offer Thanks: To our supreme God, who is worthy of all praise, honor, and glory.

Ask God: O supreme God, I pray that my child will demonstrate selfless love that is not boastful. Help him to be the kind of person described in Proverbs 27:2: "Let another praise you, and not your own mouth; someone else, and not your own lips." Help him realize that no one wants to be friends with a braggart. May he learn to hold his tongue, rather than parade his accomplishments, so he may experience the blessing of hearing praise from others — especially you, Lord. Grow in him a love that does not brag about himself but is quick to praise others. Let Christ's love restrain him from the temptation to boast. May he boast only in you, Lord. In Jesus' name, amen.

Remember: Love compels us to boast in our supreme God, not ourselves.

Guard against a Proud Spirit

Love is not ... proud. (1 Corinthians 13:4 NLT)

Praise God: Who is humble.

Confess: Every hint of pride or conceit that builds me up at the expense of others.

Offer Thanks: That God's love overflows with grace and humility.

Ask God: My humble Lord, I ask that my child would know that love is not proud. Grow in her a love that protects her from attitudes of haughtiness and conceit. Teach her that love is modest and humble, considering others to be better than herself and intentionally building up others so that she does not make anyone feel less valuable. I pray against her inflating her own importance with puffed-up arrogance. Protect her from suffering the painful consequences found in Proverbs 16:18: "Pride goes before destruction, a haughty spirit before a fall." Produce in her a humble, loving spirit like yours. In Jesus' name, amen.

Remember: God, our humble Father, is loving toward all he has made.

We Love by Serving Others, Not Ourselves

Love ... is not self-seeking. (1 Corinthians 13:4, 5)

Praise God: For he is a giving God.

Confess: Any tendency to grasp for and hold tightly to the self-serving things I want.

Offer Thanks: To my Lord for the many ways he has blessed me through his generosity.

Ask God: Dear giving Father, may my child exhibit love that is not self-seeking. May she cease from striving to get her own way through manipulation or by demanding her rights. Let her love be preoccupied with serving the needs and interests of others as she listens to their ideas and points of view. Lord, free her from the narcissistic tendencies that negatively affect so many areas of her life at home and at school. By the power of your Spirit, teach her through life experiences and your Word that love puts you first, others second, and herself last. May she be an example of your love that serves others. In Jesus' name, amen.

Remember: Our giving God is our example of love that serves others.

To Be Controlled by Love, Not Anger

Love ... is not easily angered. (1 Corinthians 13:4, 5)

Praise God: For he is merciful.

Confess: Any desire to lash out in anger rather than to show mercy.

Offer Thanks: For God's merciful heart that overflows with love for me, even when I don't deserve it.

Ask God: O most merciful Father, I ask that my child would become deeply aware of the truth that love is not easily angered. Holy Spirit, constrain him when he wants to lash out when faced with injustice or when others do not immediately respond to his demands. May he not be easily provoked by slight irritations, and may he choose to demonstrate love no matter how exasperated he is. Reveal to him how angry outbursts crush and wound the hearts of others. I pray that he will ask forgiveness and grieve over his sin of unguarded anger so that the broken relationships in his life will be healed. Grant him victory over his anger as he allows Christ's merciful, loving Spirit to control him. In Jesus' name, amen.

Remember: God is merciful and slow to anger.

True Love Is Free from the Bondage of Unforgiveness

Love … keeps no record of wrongs. (1 Corinthians 13:4, 5)

Praise God: Who is our bondage breaker.

Confess: Any times I keep score of the wounds I have received from others.

Offer Thanks: That God's powerful love not only forgives but sets me free from bondage to my past sin.

Ask God: Lord, my bondage breaker, I pray that my child will learn to love as you love by keeping no record of wrongs. I ask that she will forgive those who have wounded her deeply. May she always remember Christ's great forgiveness for her at the cross and his promise to remember her sin no more. By your mercy, may she extend that same grace to forgive others who have sinned against her. Enable her to lay down grudges, bitterness, and revenge as she refuses to keep a record of wrongs against her. O Father, please set her free from the bondage of unforgiveness. Help her to let it go. In the powerful name of Jesus, amen.

Remember: God is the bondage breaker who forgives completely and forever.

Love Rejoices in Truth, Not in Evil

Love does not delight in evil but rejoices with the truth.
(1 Corinthians 13:6)

Praise God: Who is truth.

Confess: Any inclination to delight in evil or any hesitation to rejoice in truth.

Offer Thanks: That God rejoices in truth and is faithful to lead us in following his example.

Ask God: God of all truth, may my child not delight in evil but rejoice with the truth. May he find no pleasure in evil of any kind or in gloating when others mess up or fall into sin. Teach him that love is never pleased by evil or wrongdoing but rejoices whenever truth triumphs. Reveal to him that he is always on solid footing when he stands on the truth of your Word. Keep him from compromising with the actions of others that violate your standards. Grant him a full measure of delight and joy every time your truth is victorious. In Jesus' name, amen.

Remember: Our God rejoices only in truth and hates evil.

Express God's Love through Patience

Love is patient. (1 Corinthians 13:4)

Praise God: For he is our patient God.

Confess: Any impatience in my interactions with others.

Offer Thanks: That God's love is always patient, even when we are hard-hearted and stubborn in our relationship with him.

Ask God: O most patient Father, I pray that my child will express your love for others by her patience. Please grant her the same patience in her relationships with others that you show to her. Holy Spirit, give her strength not to succumb to her natural impatience. At that moment of irritating exasperation, may she consciously pray for you to impart your patience to her. May she be determined not to show by facial expressions or curt words when the unpleasant character traits of others offend her. Let her live out Proverbs 19:11 (AMP): "Good sense makes a man restrain his anger, and it is his glory to overlook a transgression or an offense." May she be able to bear up under any situation through your loving patience. In Jesus' name, amen.

Remember: God is patient, gentle, and kind in showing his love for us.

Have a Kind Heart Like Jesus

Love is kind. (1 Corinthians 13:4)

Praise God: Who is our kind Father.

Confess: Any attitudes, thoughts, words, or actions that are unkind, demeaning, or hurtful to others.

Offer Thanks: To God for the many ways he expresses his love and kindness to us.

Ask God: O most kind Father, I pray that my child will show love to others by his kindness. Develop in him a kind heart like the heart of Jesus that spills over into acts of goodness and generous help to others without an expectation of anything in return. Father, please grow in him an attitude and lifestyle of kindness that gives up selfish pride and yields his "rights" to the Holy Spirit. I ask that you would help him learn to look for and act upon opportunities to show kindness that will bring about peace by soothing hurt feelings and calming those who are upset. May his kindness start in our home. Let his life be clothed in loving-kindness that points others to the kind, loving heart of Jesus. In Jesus' name, amen.

Remember: God is kind and loving in everything he does.

Being Truthful in Every Way

[This is what] you are to do: Speak the truth to each other.
(Zechariah 8:16)

Praise God: Who is the truth.

Confess: The times I exaggerate and am not entirely truthful with others.

Offer Thanks: To God, who is the truth and instructs us in his true and righteous ways.

Ask God: Dear God of all truth, I pray that my child will learn what he is to do: to speak the truth to others. I ask that he would act with integrity in all his ways, speaking the truth in love. Guard his mouth from saying or even intimating anything that is untruthful. May the truth he speaks to others be evidenced in his own life, and reveal to him any hidden deception or impure motives. I ask that he would walk uprightly in the truth of your Word, desiring to be obedient to all your commands. May he be known as a trustworthy man who brings glory to you wherever life takes him. In Jesus' name, amen.

Remember: God is the truth, and we can always count on him to be pure, perfect, and trustworthy.

Clothed in the Beauty of Christ

Clothe yourselves with the Lord Jesus Christ, and do not think
about how to gratify the desires of the sinful nature.
(Romans 13:14)

Praise God: Who is our Father.

Confess: The times I am not a good example in my clothing
purchases.

Offer Thanks: That our heavenly Father teaches us all of his
ways, even how to dress.

Ask God: Heavenly Father, I pray that my child will clothe
herself with the Lord Jesus Christ and not think about how to
gratify the desires of the sinful nature. She desperately wants
to fit in with the kids at school, yet so much of what is popular
to wear is not appropriate for a young woman who calls herself a Christian. Please protect her from copying the trends
and behaviors of the world. May she be more concerned about
pleasing you and reflecting the beauty of Christ than pleasing
herself or her peers. Help her realize that you care deeply about
how she looks, and you want to help her maintain perspective
in this area of her life. Remind her that she can turn to you for
help in choosing her clothes. Keep her from wearing anything
that draws sexual attention or reflects negatively on her character or yours. I sense that clothing and beauty may become
an idol for her. Turn her heart away from deceitful desires that
seek status, power, or self-esteem in outward appearance. May
she find her beauty in you. In Jesus' name, amen.

Remember: God, our heavenly Father, values inner beauty
that reflects him.

To Be a Diligent Student

Be diligent to present yourself approved to God as a workman
who does not need to be ashamed, accurately handling the word
of truth. (2 Timothy 2:15 NASB)

Praise God: Who is sovereign.

Confess: My own laziness in preparing myself to serve God.

Offer Thanks: That our sovereign God cares enough to prepare us to do the work he has planned for us.

Ask God: Sovereign Lord, I pray that my child will be diligent
to present himself approved to you as a workman who does not
need to be ashamed, accurately handling the word of truth.
Help him see that right now his work is his studies. Place a
desire in his heart for excellence and cause him to be disciplined and persistent in his study habits. May he work hard
with a good attitude to accomplish all that is required of him
so that he will not bring shame on himself by being unpre-
pared in the classroom. I pray that his teachers will not look
the other way when he is not working up to his potential but
instead will help him in any way they can when he struggles.
May he give his maximum effort in all he does, especially
being diligent in the study of your Word so that he can impart
it accurately to others. In Jesus' name, amen.

Remember: God is sovereign, helping us fulfill his plans.

Success in
Taking Tests and Exams

May the Lord our God show us his approval and make our efforts
successful. Yes, make our efforts successful!
(Psalm 90:17 NLT 1996)

Praise God: Who is all-knowing.

Confess: The times I have not valued God's approval and
have done less than my best.

Offer Thanks: For the times my all-knowing God has helped
to make my best efforts successful.

Ask God: Omniscient, all-knowing God, may you show my
child your approval and make her efforts successful. Yes,
make her efforts successful! I pray that she will turn to you
for help in understanding the material she is to study. Help
her schedule appropriate time to study for her tests. When
taking an exam, may she recall the promise that you have not
given her a spirit of fear but of power, love, and a sound mind.
Give her a calm spirit because she knows that you are there to
help her and will supernaturally bring to mind what she has
studied. I pray that she will not get sidetracked while taking
an exam, and if she is tempted to cheat, give her the integrity
and moral strength to do what is right. Whatever the outcome
of an exam, may she be at peace knowing that she did her best
and that you honor her efforts. In Jesus' name, amen.

Remember: Our all-knowing God cares enough to make our
efforts successful.

First-Day Fears

So do not fear, for I am with you. (Isaiah 41:10)

Praise God: Who is our peace.

Confess: The times I allow fear and worry to take away the peace of God's presence with me.

Offer Thanks: That the God of peace promises to be with me.

Ask God: O God of peace, may my child not fear, for you are with him. Knowing that you are with my child on his first day of school brings hope to this mother's heart. This is such a big step, and it is hard to let go. So many questions weigh heavy on my heart and mind. Will the teacher like him? Will he find good friends? Will he be tearful and afraid? Yet when I pray, placing him into your mighty, loving hands, I have peace knowing that you are right there with him. Please replace his fears with the strength and courage to face whatever the day brings. Help his teacher to be sensitive to all the little fears that walked into her classroom today. And if I could be so bold, I ask that his teacher would say something to my son that makes him feel safe and secure. Give him a real sense that Jesus is with him. In Jesus' name, amen.

Remember: God gives us his peace and his presence to calm our fears.

Desire to Be a Compassionate Witness for Christ

When [Jesus] saw the crowds, he had compassion on them, because they were harassed and helpless, like sheep without a shepherd. Then he said to his disciples, "The harvest is plentiful but the workers are few. Ask the Lord of the harvest, therefore, to send out workers into his harvest field." (Matthew 9:36–38)

Praise God: Who is Lord of the harvest.

Confess: Any hardness of heart that keeps me from caring about harassed and helpless people who do not know Jesus.

Offer Thanks: That I know Jesus as my Savior and Lord because he had compassion on me.

Ask God: Lord of the harvest, when my child sees the crowds on his school campus, may he have compassion on them, for they are harassed and helpless, like sheep without a shepherd. The harvest is plentiful, but the workers are few. Therefore, I ask you, Lord of the harvest, to open my son's eyes to see that he is a worker sent to the harvest field of his school. Give him the compassion of Jesus for his fellow students. Without fear and with a loving, gracious heart, may he share his faith with those who do not know you. Help him tell the story of his Savior, who redeemed him and changed his life forever. May he be a faithful messenger of your grace to the children and staff members he encounters. In the name of Jesus, our Savior and Redeemer, amen.

Remember: The Lord of the harvest desires that not one sheep would be lost.

Being a Witness
of the Word of Life

Become blameless and pure, children of God without fault in a
crooked and depraved generation, in which you shine like stars in
the universe as you hold out the word of life. (Philippians 2:15–16)

Praise God: Who is the Word of Life.

Confess: The times my unconfessed sin darkens the light of
God's life within me.

Offer Thanks: That the Word of Life transforms the crooked
and depraved into pure and blameless shining stars.

Ask God: O blessed Word of Life, I pray that my child will
become blameless and pure, a child of God without fault in
a crooked and depraved generation. May he shine like a star
in the universe as he holds out the Word of Life to those who
do not know you. May he never be ashamed of the gospel of
Christ, because it is the power of God unto salvation for all
who believe. I cry out for a spiritual awakening and revival on
my son's campus. Help him and others who love you to be the
purified, sanctified vessels you can use to change his campus
for Christ. In your mercy, Lord, save this depraved and hopeless generation for your glory. In Jesus' name, amen.

Remember: Our God, the Word of life, makes his children
shine like stars in the universe.

Praying for Classmates and Teachers Who Don't Know Jesus

Therefore I tell you, whatever you ask for in prayer, believe that you have received it, and it will be yours. (Mark 11:24)

Praise God: Who is faithful.

Confess: Any weakness of faith or lack of trust that leads me to doubt God's faithfulness.

Offer Thanks: For God's faithfulness in responding to my prayers for big, important things.

Ask God: O Father who is faithful, I pray for my child to believe that whatever she asks for in prayer, she has received it, and it will be hers. I ask that you would pour out your Spirit of prayer upon her to cry out for the lost at her school. May she know that praying for her classmates and teachers is the most important thing she can do. Please bring others who will join with her in praying that you will open the eyes of the blind and turn them from darkness to light and from the power of Satan to God so that they may receive forgiveness for their sins and a place among those who are sanctified by faith. Assure her of your promise that you are patient, not wanting anyone to perish but wanting everyone to come to repentance. Put a great expectation on her heart that her prayers are making a difference. In Jesus' name, amen.

Remember: God is faithful to keep all his promises.

Protection
from Physical Harm

[God] orders his angels to protect you wherever you go.
(Psalm 91:11 NLT 1996)

Praise God: Our protector.

Confess: The fear that God will allow my child to slip out of his protective care.

Offer Thanks: That my child is never out of God's sight and protective care.

Ask God: O blessed Protector, I pray that you will order your angels to protect my child wherever he goes. He is so rambunctious and does things before he thinks about what the consequences might be. I cry out to you for his physical protection today. It is a great comfort to know that you command your angels to deliver him from harmful activities and protect him from injury. Please help him to make the right choice about things he should and should not do. Tame his impulsiveness. Strengthen him to not heed the persuasive cheers or mocking taunts of friends who challenge him to take daring risks. May he find comfort in knowing that your angels are with him to guide and protect him. In Jesus' name, amen.

Remember: God is always our protector in the physical and the spiritual realms.

Choosing a College

The LORD says, "I will guide you along the best pathway for your life. I will advise you and watch over you." (Psalm 32:8 NLT 1996)

Praise God: Who is our Counselor.

Confess: Any fear or pride that pushes me to try to manipulate and control my child's future.

Offer Thanks: That my child's future is in God's able hands, and that he will guide her in the best pathway.

Ask God: O blessed Counselor, I cry out for my child's heart to be at peace because she can trust you to guide her along the best pathway for her life. May she find confidence in knowing that you will advise her and watch over her. Help her research different colleges and universities and evaluate them rightly. Give her a heart that seeks your counsel first and welcomes godly counsel from others as she makes this most important decision. May she not heed voices that are contrary to yours. Please give a clear indication of where she should go, and close the door to universities or colleges that would not be good for her. I ask that she would find godly fellowship in a vibrant Christian ministry on her campus. May it be a place where she can get involved and develop her gifts and talents as she grows in her faith. In Jesus' name, amen.

Remember: God, our Counselor, advises, guides, and watches over us.

Protection from Drinking

Wine produces mockers; liquor leads to brawls. Whoever is led astray by drink cannot be wise. (Proverbs 20:1 NLT 1996)

Praise God: Who is trustworthy.

Confess: The times I have a casual attitude toward God's clear warnings.

Offer Thanks: That God's warnings are true, and that he will protect us from harm.

Ask God: O trustworthy Father, I pray that my child will wisely heed the warning that wine produces mockers and liquor leads to brawls. May she realize that whoever is led astray by drink cannot be wise. I ask you to protect her from being squeezed into the world's mold that allows alcohol to be acceptable and available, tempting and luring kids like her. Grant her insight to see beyond the media's glamorization of social drinking. May she be careful to make decisions that would keep her from precarious situations where she could be tempted to give in or be taken advantage of. Impart courage to her to resist temptation, and empower her daily to obey your command to not be drunk with alcohol. Protect her from giving any ground to the Enemy, who is out to destroy her body, mind, and spirit. Instead, may she be filled with and controlled by your Spirit to drink of the abundance of your grace, quenching her thirst from your river of delights. In Jesus' name, amen.

Remember: God's words of warning are always trustworthy.

Wisdom in Choosing Friends

Oh, the joys of those who do not follow the advice of the wicked, or stand around with sinners, or join in with scoffers. But they delight in doing everything the LORD wants; day and night they think about his law. They are like trees planted along the riverbank, bearing fruit each season without fail. Their leaves never wither, and in all they do, they prosper. (Psalm 1:1–3 NLT 1996)

Praise God: Who is wise.

Confess: Any carelessness in choosing how or with whom I spend my time.

Offer Thanks: That God's Word brings joy into my life when I obey its wisdom.

Ask God: Wise heavenly Father, I pray for my child to live in the joy of not following the advice of the wicked, or standing around with sinners, or joining in with scoffers. May he delight in doing everything you want; day and night may he think about your law. Then he will be like a tree planted along the riverbank, bearing fruit each season without fail, not withering but prospering in all he does. O Father, may he choose to walk with the wise rather than foolish, godless companions. Guide him to relationships that draw him closer to you. I pray that his heart will be attracted to those who love you and not to those who may be popular or outwardly attractive but despise the things you love. Lead my son to seek you with a pure heart that delights in your commands, so that he will prosper. In Jesus' name, amen.

Remember: God is wise, and his ways bring joy to those who walk in them.

Wisdom in Prioritizing Time

Seek first [God's] kingdom and his righteousness, and all these things will be given to you as well. (Matthew 6:33)

Praise God: Who provides.

Confess: The times when God's priorities take second place as I strive to fulfill my own desires.

Offer Thanks: That God graciously and generously provides for those who seek to obey him above all else.

Ask God: O blessed Provider, I ask that my child would seek first your kingdom and righteousness, and all other things will be given to her as well. O Lord, may she know that when she puts you first, you will provide everything she needs. So many activities are vying for her time and attention, and she needs your discernment to spend her time wisely. She has a tendency to take on too much, which causes her great anxiety. So I pray that she will learn to ask you for wisdom in setting priorities. Whenever she wants to add a new activity to her already busy schedule, may she listen to your voice and obey. Give her joy in knowing that obedience brings blessing. Grant her a calm, peaceful spirit, trusting that you have the best pathway planned for her life. In Jesus' name, amen.

Remember: God provides the best for those who seek to please him.

Winning Favor from Coaches and Teammates

Let love and faithfulness never leave you; bind them around your neck, write them on the tablet of your heart. Then you will win favor and a good name in the sight of God and man. (Proverbs 3:3–4)

Praise God: For his extravagant love.

Confess: The times when my love waxes cold.

Offer Thanks: That God delights in love and wants us to be known for love and faithfulness.

Ask God: Dear loving Father, I pray that love and faithfulness will never leave my child; bind them around his neck, write them on the tablet of his heart. Then he will win favor and a good name in the sight of God and people. Lord, you have blessed my son with divine favor among his teammates and coaches. May he be thankful for this honor and have a keen sense of responsibility to act like Christ as a person of integrity, love, and kindness. May he be faithful to work hard, and help him look for ways to encourage, build up, and strengthen his team. Protect him from the temptation to curse, demean, or ridicule others. Whether his team wins or loses, may his first response be to give you glory and not focus on the acclaim that his success in sports gives him. I pray that the love and faithfulness of his character would be so winsome that he would be a clear witness of Christ, who lives in him. In Jesus' name, amen.

Remember: Love and faithfulness delight the heart of God.

Guard against Prejudice

[God] has showed you, O man, what is good. And what does the LORD require of you? To act justly and to love mercy and to walk humbly with your God. (Micah 6:8)

Praise God: Who is just.

Confess: The times when pride becomes more important to me than justice and mercy.

Offer Thanks: That our just God shows us how to do what is good.

Ask God: O just Father, I pour out my heart asking that my child would do what is good and what you require of her: to act justly and love mercy and walk humbly with her God. Help her remember that you created every person, and that you love all the people of the world. I pray that she will do what is good in your eyes and be humble, fair, and merciful toward the people she encounters every day. May she see with your eyes those who are different from her. Keep her from being unkind or prideful toward people who need help. May she comfort the forsaken, befriend the lonely, show love to the timid, lift up the weak, include the outsider, speak a kind word to the unpopular and unattractive, and be fair to all. Loving Father, I pray that prejudice will have no part in her life. Bless her as she seeks to please you in doing what is good and right. In Jesus' name, amen.

Remember: God is just and merciful and wants us to do what is good.

Showing Respect to Teachers

Show respect for all men [treat them honorably]. (1 Peter 2:17 AMP)

Praise God: Who is our Lord and Master.

Confess: The times I dishonor God by disrespecting people he created.

Offer Thanks: That God, my Lord and Master, chooses to honor me.

Ask God: O Lord and Master, I ask that my child would show respect for everyone and treat them honorably, including his teacher. Help my son realize that you created his teacher in your image, and that you love and value his teacher just as you love and value him. May he show proper respect by graciously obeying what his teacher asks of him, even if he doesn't like it. Help him refrain from dishonorable behavior, such as talking back or whispering demeaning things about his teacher. Give him courage to refuse to join in with classmates who want to mock or belittle their teacher. May he not only be courteous and polite but desire to pray for his teacher, because you have chosen this teacher for him for a purpose, and you never make mistakes. In Jesus' name, amen.

Remember: God, our Lord and Master, wants us to be respectful and treat everyone honorably.

Safety on Trips

The LORD watches over you.... The LORD will keep you from all harm — he will watch over your life; the LORD will watch over your coming and going both now and forevermore. (Psalm 121:5, 7, 8)

Praise God: Who is watchful.

Confess: My tendency to worry about my child's safety.

Offer Thanks: To God, who promises to watch over us now and forever.

Ask God: O watchful God, I pray, watch over my child. Keep him from all harm — watch over his life. Watch over his coming and going both now and forevermore. As he goes on this trip, I pray for safe travel. Keep the drivers alert and help them make good decisions on the road. Lord, you know my son, so I ask that he would act in a responsible manner. Help him listen to and obey the instructions he is given and make wise decisions along the way. Please command your angels to guard him everywhere he goes and keep him from being harmed or hurt in any way. I pray this also for his travel companions. May this be a wonderful trip without incident, a trip that will bring many fond memories. In Jesus' name, amen.

Remember: God watches over us always.

Do Not Give Up Doing Good

Let us not become weary in doing good, for at the proper time we will reap a harvest if we do not give up. (Galatians 6:9)

Praise God: Who is all-sufficient.

Confess: The times I deliberately choose not to do what I know is good.

Offer Thanks: That God promises a harvest for doing good.

Ask God: My all-sufficient Father, I ask that my child would not become weary in doing good, for at the proper time he will reap a harvest if he does not give up. When he feels like giving up, I pray that you will strengthen his hands and steady his knees. When he thinks he can't study one more page, or run one more lap, or resist temptation one more minute, I ask that he would come to his all-sufficient Jesus for help. Please assure him that you hear his cries and will graciously answer his prayers. Thank you that you will provide all he needs to keep doing what is right. Help him not to give up and miss out on the harvest that is waiting to be revealed. In Jesus' name, amen.

Remember: God is sufficient to meet our needs when we are weary.

Wisdom to Walk in God's Ways

> He who trusts in himself is a fool, but he who walks in wisdom is kept safe. (Proverbs 28:26)

Praise God: Who is wise.

Confess: The times I think of myself as wise enough to walk in my own wisdom.

Offer Thanks: That God generously gives us wisdom to protect us from being foolish.

Ask God: O God of wisdom, I pray that my child will recognize the truth that he who trusts in himself is a fool, but he who walks in wisdom is kept safe. Lord, you have gifted him greatly, and others are recognizing those gifts in his life. I ask that you would keep him from falling into the trap of arrogance that harms the character of so many able, young men. I see hints of foolish pride creeping into his attitudes, and I ask that you would compel him to take captive every thought that crosses his mind and purify it through the holy wisdom of your Word. Teach him to walk in your ways so that he will be kept safe in the shelter of your wisdom. In Jesus' name, amen.

Remember: God is wise in all his ways.

Protection from Drug Use

You are my refuge and my shield; I have put my hope in your word. (Psalm 119:114)

Praise God: Who is mighty.

Confess: The times I am afraid for my child and put my hope in anything but the mighty power of God and his Word.

Offer Thanks: That I have hope because God is able to protect my child.

Ask God: O mighty God, I cry out to you that my child would turn to you as his refuge and shield, putting his hope in your Word. I pray that nothing would rob him of the abundant life you have purposed for him. Right now, peer pressure, difficult studies, and self-image issues are causing him to feel uncertain and insecure. I ask that he would find his refuge in you instead of drugs. Make him wise to Satan's lies that drugs are the answer. May he see that those who use drugs and entice him to do the same are walking in darkness, headed down a road of dissolution, sickness, and destruction. Help him trust that you will be with him — a protective wall of fire against any evil influences — when he is tempted. Give him courage to say no so that he will not compromise his faith. May he stand firm in all the will of God, desiring to please you in all he does. In Jesus' name I pray, amen.

Remember: God is mighty to be our protector, our refuge, our shield, and our hope.

For Release from
Drug and Alcohol Addiction

[May the enslaved] come to their senses and escape from the
trap of the devil, who has taken them captive to do his will.
(2 Timothy 2:26)

Praise God: For he is able.

Confess: Any addictions that ensnare me, causing me to need
God's deliverance.

Offer Thanks: That our merciful God is able to deliver us from
the Devil's many traps.

Ask God: I cry out to you, merciful Savior, that my enslaved
child would come to his senses and escape from the trap of the
Devil, who has taken him captive to do his will. My heart is in
deep anguish over the devastating toll this addiction has taken
in my son's life. In Jesus' powerful name, demolish this stronghold that keeps him trapped in such a dark, hopeless place.
Do whatever it takes, Lord, for him to repent and surrender
his life to you. Open his eyes to the truth: he is enslaved and
helpless to control his addiction. May your great love break
through Satan's lies that tell my son he is fine or needs this
substance to survive. I pray earnestly for him day and night,
Lord Jesus, trusting in your power to deliver him. Give me
wisdom to know what to do next, keep me from enabling his
destructive behavior, and help me live in your promise that
you will work all things together for his good and your glory.
Humble me to ask others to pray for my son's deliverance. I
pray for victory in the mighty name of Jesus, amen.

Remember: God is able to deliver and is faithful in mercy.

Transforming
a Prideful, Contentious Spirit

By pride comes nothing but [contention]. (Proverbs 13:10 NKJV)

Praise God: Who is able.

Confess: Any pride or other negative character traits that might contribute to quarrels.

Offer Thanks: That God is able to save us from attitudes and behaviors that harm our relationships.

Ask God: O Father who is able, I ask you to show my child that nothing but contention comes from pride. Please open her eyes to see that our home is often a war zone because of her contentious conduct. Convict her that her quarrelsome, antagonistic, argumentative, cranky, combative, and belligerent behavior stems from a prideful heart. By the power of your grace, help her deny her selfish impulses and surrender to Jesus. I pray that she would confess her sin, repent, and humbly seek forgiveness from those she has wronged. When she is tempted to lash out, may she immediately turn to you and pray for self-control. And when I am tempted to respond to her behavior in anger, may I humbly turn to you for wisdom in what I say and do. By the power of your Word and prayer, transform her prideful, contentious heart to a humble, loving heart. Father, you are able to tear down this stronghold in her life, so I ask you to renew her mind and conform her to the image of your Son. In the powerful name of Jesus, amen.

Remember: God is able to transform us into the likeness of his Son, Jesus.

Protection from Willful Disobedience

Keep back Your servant from presumptuous sins; let them not rule over me. (Psalm 19:13 NASB)

Praise God: Who is holy.

Confess: Any stubbornness of heart that keeps me from obeying God's commands.

Offer Thanks: That our holy God delivers us from enslavement to sin.

Ask God: O holy God, I cry out for my child that you would keep her back from presumptuous sins; let them not rule over her. Please reveal to her the seriousness of her willful sins. From early childhood she has been taught your ways, yet she deliberately chooses to go contrary to the teachings she has learned and indulge in sin. She is in a downward spiral, chasing her own desires and putting herself in authority rather than you. Please take away the attitudes of arrogance, insolence, and brazen defiance against your will and your Word. Help her listen to her conscience before she no longer hears the promptings of the Holy Spirit. Rescue her; pull her out of the miry pit of her self-willed, stubborn heart. Lord, by your divine mercy, break her will and grant her sorrowful repentance so that she turns back to you, for the praise of your glory. In Jesus' name, amen.

Remember: Our holy God wants us to be free from bondage to sin.

To Be Humble
in All Relationships

Show true humility to everyone. (Titus 3:2 NLT)

Praise God: Who is humble.

Confess: The times I allow pride to stand in the way of asking for forgiveness and forgiving others.

Offer Thanks: That Jesus, being God, humbled himself to die a criminal's death on the cross for my sins.

Ask God: My humble Lord, I pray that my child will show true humility toward everyone. I ask that you would conform his heart to the likeness of the humble heart of Jesus. Cultivate in him the desire to live in a spirit of sincere humility. When he is successful, I pray that he would be grateful but not boast in himself. When he does wrong, I ask that he would readily admit his mistake and not try to justify himself or blame something or someone else. May he esteem others for their accomplishments with sincere happiness on their behalf. May he experience joy as he builds others up in a spirit of humility rather than building himself up in a spirit of pride. For your glory, in Jesus' name, amen.

Remember: God is humble, with no hint of pride.

For a Dating Relationship

Love must be sincere. Hate what is evil; cling to what is good.
Be devoted to one another in brotherly love. Honor one another
above yourselves. (Romans 12:9–10)

Praise God: For he is Lord.

Confess: The times my love for my Lord and others lacks sincerity, devotion, and honor.

Offer Thanks: That God teaches us how to honor him as Lord.

Ask God: Lord, let my child's love be sincere. Cause her to hate what is evil and cling to what is good. Let her be devoted to others in brotherly love, honoring others above herself. Lord, in my daughter's dating relationships, I ask that she would be wise and choose young men who love you, who are respectful of her, and who think of her welfare more than their own desires. I ask that the Holy Spirit protect her from being taken advantage of and give her strength to say no. When she becomes involved in a dating relationship, I ask for your hand of protection to be on both of them. May their growing attraction for each other be directed by their faithful relationship with you and their sincere desire to honor one another. May they guard their hearts, holding strong to purity of heart and behavior as they spend time together and get to know each other. O Lord, I pray that they would honor you above all else, and that they might honor one another. In Jesus' name, amen.

Remember: God is our Lord and Master.

For My Daughter's Future Husband

"You shall love the LORD your God with all your heart, and with all your soul, and with all your mind, and with all your strength." The second [command] is this, "You shall love your neighbor as yourself." There is no other commandment greater than these. (Mark 12:30–31 NASB)

Praise God: Who is sovereign.

Confess: Any priorities for my daughter's future husband that are outside God's will.

Offer Thanks: To our sovereign God, who is the blessed controller of all things.

Ask God: Sovereign God, I pray that my daughter's future husband will love you with all his heart, soul, mind, and strength, and love his neighbor as himself. I ask that she would not be yoked with an unbeliever (2 Corinthians 6:14). May they honor the marriage bed and keep it pure (Hebrews 13:4). May her future husband be considerate and treat her with respect so that nothing will hinder his prayers (1 Peter 3:7). May he love her as Christ loved the church and gave himself up for her (Ephesians 5:25). I ask that he would be humble, gentle, and patient, keeping the bond of peace (Ephesians 4:2–3). May he seek your kingdom first, knowing you will give him all he needs to be a godly father and a good provider (Matthew 6:33; Ephesians 6:4; 1 Timothy 5:8). Lord, may my daughter wait patiently for you to lead her to this man of godly character. I ask that their entire household would love and serve you. In Jesus' name, amen.

Remember: God's sovereign desires for us are good.

For My Son's Future Wife

"You shall love the LORD your God with all your heart, and with all your soul, and with all your mind, and with all your strength." The second [command] is this, "You shall love your neighbor as yourself." There is no other commandment greater than these. (Mark 12:30–31 NASB)

Praise God: Who is sovereign.

Confess: Any priorities for my son's future wife that are outside God's will.

Offer Thanks: To our sovereign God, who is the blessed controller of all things.

Ask God: Sovereign God, I pray that my son's future wife will love the Lord her God with all her heart, and with all her soul, and with all her mind, and with all her strength, and that she will her neighbor as herself. I pray that my son will not be yoked with an unbeliever (2 Corinthians 6:14). May they honor the marriage bed and keep it pure (Hebrews 13:4). I ask that his future wife would submit to him, as to the Lord (Ephesians 5:22). May she bring him good and not harm all the days of her life (Proverbs 31:12). I pray that she will work energetically to care for her household, and that kindness would be the rule of her mouth (Proverbs 31). May she respect him (Ephesians 5:33) and be completely humble, gentle, patient, and loving (Ephesians 4:2–3). Lord, may my son wait patiently for you to lead him to this woman of godly character. I ask that their entire household would love and serve you. In Jesus' name, amen.

Remember: God's sovereign desires for us are good.

To Leave a Legacy of Faith

Know therefore that the LORD your God is God; he is the faithful
God, keeping his covenant of love to a thousand generations of
those who love him and keep his commands. (Deuteronomy 7:9)

Praise God: Who is eternal.

Confess: The challenges I have in keeping my commitment
to walk with God.

Offer Thanks: That God is faithful to keep his promises not
just to me but to my children who walk with him.

Ask God: Eternal God, I pray for my child to believe this
promise and fulfill its requirements: that you, O Lord, are
God; you are the faithful God, keeping your covenant of love
to a thousand generations of those who love you and keep your
commands. I ask that my son would be careful to love you and
keep your commands so that his legacy of faith will be passed
down generationally to his offspring until you come. I pray
against weak faith and ask that my son be intentional about
telling of your mighty works and praising your greatness to
his children. May he find planned and unplanned opportunities for spiritual conversation and study with them. In your
mercy I ask that not one of his children, grandchildren, or
great-grandchildren would be lost. Redeem them; call them
by name. May your hand be upon them to fulfill the destiny
you have ordained for their lives before the foundation of the
world. In Jesus' name, amen.

Remember: God is eternally faithful not just for today but
forever.

Learning to Give Thanks

Continue to live in [Jesus], rooted and built up in him, strengthened in the faith as you were taught, and overflowing with thankful-ness.... Give thanks in all circumstances, for this is God's will for you in Christ Jesus. (Colossians 2:6–7; 1 Thessalonians 5:18)

Praise God: Who is good.

Confess: The times my heart does not overflow with thanks to God.

Offer Thanks: To God, who is good and is the giver of every good thing we receive.

Ask God: Dear good God, I pray that my child will continue to live in you, rooted and built up in you, strengthened in the faith as she was taught, and overflowing with thankfulness. I ask that she would give thanks in all circumstances, for this is your will for her in Christ Jesus. Father, develop in her a heart of thankfulness. May giving thanks become a life-changing habit that produces a quiet spirit that gives thanks and does not grumble, complain, or indulge in self-pity. Help her experience joy in giving thanks in all circumstances. When her prayers are answered, I ask that she would acknowledge with thanks that you answered them. Increase her faith to believe that your commands are always for her good. Build up her faith to trust you and give thanks for prayers you have not yet answered. May she trust in your plan and perfect timing because she knows that you are good all the time. In Jesus' name, amen.

Remember: God is good and wills that we overflow with thanksgiving.

For Protection When Driving

He will give His angels charge concerning you, to guard you in all your ways. (Psalm 91:11 NASB)

Praise God: Who is captain of the heavenly host.

Confess: Any doubt of God's power to protect my children.

Offer Thanks: That God commands angels to protect us.

Ask God: Captain of the heavenly host, I praise you for the promise that you will give your angels charge concerning my child, to guard him in all his ways. Lord, now that my son is driving, I pray for your mighty hand of protection on his comings and goings. Please give him healthy fear and sound judgment in how he drives, because he loves the feeling of power when he presses that gas pedal. Don't let him drive like a maniac, show off to siblings or peers, drink alcohol, or text. May he choose to obey and honor you by respecting and obeying the law. In that split second when he does not make good decisions, Lord, send your ministering angels to surround his car. Protect him and bring him safely to his destination. Whenever he gets behind the wheel, may he remember that driving is a privilege and responsibility, and that the decisions he makes could be matters of life and death not only for himself but also for others. In Jesus' name, amen.

Remember: As captain of the heavenly host, God has the power to protect us.

To Be Caught When Guilty

Be sure that your sin will find you out.... It was good for me to
be afflicted so that I might learn your decrees. (Numbers 32:23;
Psalm 119:71)

Praise God: Who is everywhere.

Confess: The sins I think are insignificant in God's sight.

Offer Thanks: That God is always present and loves me so
much that he will not allow me to hide my sin from him.

Ask God: O omnipresent God, I pray that my child would
know for sure that his sin will find him out. May he say that
it was good for him to be afflicted so that he might learn your
decrees. Father, you are everywhere and see everything. I ask
that if my son is doing wrong, you would not allow him to get
away with it. May he know that because of your great love for
him, you will expose his sin. When this happens, I ask that
he would repent with godly sorrow that leads to healing, restoration, and forgiveness. Even though being afflicted in this
way is painful and the consequences could be severe, I pray
that he will learn from this correction and not go back to the
sin again. Lord, even if it my breaks my heart, allow him to be
caught so that the joy of his salvation can be restored and his
guilt erased. In Jesus' name, amen.

Remember: God is everywhere, revealing hidden sin and
watching over us to help us learn his ways.

Disciplined for Our Good

God disciplines us for our good, that we may share in his holiness. No discipline seems pleasant at the time, but painful. Later on, however, it produces a harvest of righteousness and peace for those who have been trained by it. (Hebrews 12:10–11)

Praise God: Who is our heavenly Father.

Confess: My shortsighted view of God's discipline in my life.

Offer Thanks: That God willingly trains even my stubborn heart to share in his holiness.

Ask God: Heavenly Father, please help my child realize that you discipline him for his good, that he may share in your holiness. No discipline seems pleasant at the time but painful. Later on, however, it will produce a harvest of righteousness and peace in his life as he is trained by it. May he understand that your discipline is proof of your deep love for him. May he not rebel but submit to your discipline with a repentant heart. Show him that what you allow in his life is intended to draw him closer to you and conform him to the image of Christ. Train him by your Word to discern truth from error and holy behavior from unholy. Give him an earnest desire to walk in your ways so that he may fulfill your mighty calling on his life. May he believe that your perfect discipline is always for his good and that you will not give him more than he can bear. Produce in him an abundant harvest of righteousness and peace. In Jesus' name, amen.

Remember: Our heavenly Father disciplines us for our good and his purpose.

Using One's Spiritual Gift

As each one has received a special gift, employ it in serving one another as good stewards of the manifold grace of God. (1 Peter 4:10 NASB)

Praise God: For his grace.

Confess: The times I have withheld my God-given spiritual gift and not served others as he desires.

Offer Thanks: That God counts me worthy to receive a special gift from him to serve and bless others.

Ask God: O Father of grace, you have given my child a special gift. I ask that she would employ it in serving others as a good steward of your manifold grace. Bless her to believe that the Holy Spirit has given her a supernatural ability designed just for her. May knowing this make her feel very special and loved by you. Grant her wisdom to know what her special gift is, and make me aware of where she shines so that I might encourage her in the gift you have given. I pray that she will take her God-given gift seriously and be faithful to use it to further your kingdom. Please open doors of opportunity so that she might serve you with joy. Empower her by your Holy Spirit to manifest all the gifts, abilities, and talents you have given her to serve and build up the body of Christ for your glory. In Jesus' name, amen.

Remember: By his grace, God gives each of us a gift to serve others.

Developing a Desire to Worship God

Shout for joy to the LORD, all the earth. Worship the LORD with gladness; come before him with joyful songs. (Psalm 100:1–2)

Praise God: Who is joy.

Confess: The times I go through the motions and don't worship God from my heart.

Offer Thanks: That God delights to hear our joyful worship.

Ask God: O God of joy, I ask that my child would use her heart and voice to shout for joy to the Lord with all the earth. May she worship you with gladness and come before you with joyful songs. Lord, you delight in our worship, and I pray that my child will also delight in worshipping you. I pray that the songs that come from her lips will be joyful songs of praise to you. May her greatest desire be to worship you in the quiet of the morning (Psalm 59:16; 90:14), in her daily activities (Psalm 35:28; 71:8; 89:16), in her bed at night (Psalm 63:6; 92:2), and in the company of your saints (Psalm 27:4). As she grows in her relationship with you, may she be filled with praises in her heart and give voice to songs of joy and gladness. In Jesus' name, amen.

Remember: God is our joy, worthy of our praise and worship.

Commitment to What Really Matters

Remember, O LORD, how I have walked before you faithfully and with wholehearted devotion and have done what is good in your eyes. (Isaiah 38:3)

Praise God: Who sanctifies.

Confess: The times I have not been faithful to follow Christ.

Offer Thanks: That God knows all of my successes and failures and has not given up on me.

Ask God: My God who sanctifies, I ask that my child would walk before you faithfully and with wholehearted devotion, doing what is good in your eyes. Develop in him the character of commitment. Empower him by the Holy Spirit to be resolute, unrelenting, and disciplined to seek you first and commit to your lordship. May he commit to study your Word daily and pray without ceasing so that he will follow you all the days of his life. May he commit all his ways, time, talent, and resources to you. May he be steadfast in his commitment to you even in the face of adverse circumstances, rejection, and criticism. I pray for him Jesus' prayer in John 17:11: "Holy Father, protect him by the power of your name." May he have the full measure of your joy. Please strengthen his sacrificial commitment so that he might experience the abundant life that only you can give. In Jesus' name, amen.

Remember: God sanctifies us to walk faithfully with him.

Protection from Obesity and Eating Disorders

Do you not know that your body is a temple of the Holy Spirit, who is in you, whom you have received from God? You are not your own; you were bought at a price. Therefore honor God with your body. (1 Corinthians 6:19–20)

Praise God: Who is love.

Confess: Any behavior that is harmful to the body God has given me.

Offer Thanks: That God paid a tremendous price so that we could belong to him.

Ask God: O loving God, I pray that my child will know that her body is a temple of the Holy Spirit, who is in her, whom she received from you. May she realize that she is not her own; you bought her at a price. Therefore, may she honor you with her body. Lord, teach her to make healthy food choices, and help me to model a healthy lifestyle for her. When she feels pressure to be thin and compares herself with others, remind her that she is beautiful in your sight, fearfully and wonderfully made. When she feels the obsessive-compulsive need to medicate herself with food, may she cry out to you for help. Fill her instead with the controlling power and loving presence of your Spirit. Give her discipline to maintain a healthy weight, and protect her from destructive behaviors that would rob her of health and life. May she see herself through your eyes and value the beauty of her love relationship with you most of all. In Jesus' name, amen.

Remember: Our loving God values us so highly that he chooses us to be his temple.

For God's Love to Intervene and Prevent Self-Harm

May your roots go down deep into the soil of God's marvelous love. And may you have the power to understand . . . how wide, how long, how high, and how deep his love really is. (Ephesians 3:17–18 NLT 1996)

Praise God: Who is love.

Confess: The times I doubt God's immeasurable love for me.

Offer Thanks: That God's love for me is so much greater than I could ever imagine.

Ask God: Loving Father, may my child's roots go down deep into the soil of your marvelous love. May she have the power to understand how wide, how long, how high, and how deep your love really is. Father, when I found out that she was inflicting harm on her body, I was devastated. I don't understand why she is doing this, but I pray that you would heal whatever is causing this self-destructive behavior. Set her mind free from wrong thinking. Open her eyes to see that this behavior comes from the Enemy, who is robbing her of joy and health. Pull her out of this pit of anger, rejection, and hurt. Show me how to love and help her. Grant me grace to keep praying for her and not give up. Lead us to a Christian counselor who can shed light on the agony and deception in her soul. May her identity become firmly rooted in your unconditional, immeasurable, and marvelous love. In Jesus' name, amen.

Remember: The love of God has no limits.

Releasing Burdens
to God's Care

Cast your cares on the LORD and he will sustain you; he will never let the righteous fall. (Psalm 55:22)

Praise God: Who is my strength.

Confess: The times I insist on bearing my own burdens instead of relinquishing them and depending on God's sustaining power.

Offer Thanks: That God cares enough to help us bear life's burdens.

Ask God: O mighty Lord who is my strength, I pray that my child will cast her cares on you. I ask that you will sustain her and never let her fall. Lord, she is held captive by the wrong thinking that she has to have it all together all the time. I see her suffering from the burden of fear, worry, and anxiety that comes with this thinking, yet she is trying desperately to maintain control. I fear that this will result in great harm for her. So I ask, caring Father, for you to lead her to your Word so that she will hear your tender, loving voice saying, "Come to me, my child; you are carrying heavy burdens. I am able to take them and give you peace. Give them to me." Through the strength of your love and grace, help her to cast all her cares on you. In Jesus' name, amen.

Remember: God is strong and powerful to sustain us.

Protection from Suicide

My frame was not hidden from you when I was made in the secret place. When I was woven together in the depths of the earth, your eyes saw my unformed body. All the days ordained for me were written in your book before one of them came to be. (Psalm 139:15–16)

Praise God: Who is our creator.

Confess: Any thinking that God does not know me, love me, or care for me.

Offer Thanks: That God created me, and it was good.

Ask God: O creator God, I praise you that my child's frame was not hidden from you when you made her in the secret place. When she was woven together in the depths of the earth, your eyes saw her unformed body. All the days ordained for her were written in your book before one of them came to be. O God, my child is in unbearable pain. She is consumed with despair and thinks her life is so worthless, meaningless, and messed up that she wants to end it. Father, you have known my precious child since before I carried her in my womb. You have a plan for her life, a purpose for each of her days. I plead with you to drive away her despair and restore her hope by the power of your Spirit. May she find her hope in you, Lord. Protect her and heal her distorted thinking. Give her doctors and counselors wisdom in treating her. Preserve her life, Lord, for your glory and her good. In Jesus' name, amen.

Remember: God our Creator has ordained every day of our lives.

Healing for a Loss
Due to Suicide

The Spirit of God has made me; the breath of the Almighty gives me life. (Job 33:4)

Praise God: Who is the giver of life.

Confess: The times I grieve God because I do not want to live.

Offer Thanks: To God, who made me and whose very breath gives me life.

Ask God: O God of life, I pray that my child will realize his great value, knowing that the Spirit of God made him; the breath of the Almighty gives him life. May he comprehend just how precious this gift of life is, even as he grieves the loss of a loved one to suicide. In his anguish and confusion, I pray that you would protect and comfort his grieving heart. He does not understand how someone he cared about could do such a tragic thing. Help him pour out his fear, sorrow, anger, guilt, and feelings of betrayal to you. May he trust you with all of his unanswered questions and find hope and solace in your love. Remind him that you understand his grief and pain because you lost your only Son — Jesus, our Redeemer. Help him recognize the seeds of redemption in this devastating loss and to see glimpses of your glory. Grant him deep compassion for this loved one and empower him to minister your comfort, love, and hope to others. In Jesus' name, amen.

Remember: God is the God of life and hope.

Learn the
Secret of Contentment

I have learned the secret of contentment in every situation,
whether it be a full stomach or hunger, plenty or want.
(Philippians 4:12–13 TLB)

Praise God: Who provides.

Confess: Any grumbling regarding God's provision that leads
me to have an ungrateful heart.

Offer Thanks: That God always and generously provides for
me.

Ask God: My Lord who provides, I ask that my child would
learn the secret of contentment in every situation, whether it
be a full stomach or hunger, plenty or want. Lord, you have
given contentment not as a gift but as something you want
us to learn. So I pray that he will have a receptive heart as
you teach him how to be content in all circumstances. Cause
him to remember that you promise to provide for all of his
needs — material, physical, mental, and spiritual — through
Christ's great riches. Give him a deep sense of gratitude and
contentment with what you have provided for him. May he
realize that complaining and grumbling stem from a discontented, unthankful heart, which is sin. Fill him with a loving,
trusting heart that is content in every situation because he is
satisfied in his relationship with you. In Jesus' name, amen.

Remember: God provides all we need.

Guard against Greed

Watch out! Be on your guard against all kinds of greed; a man's life does not consist in the abundance of his possessions. (Luke 12:15)

Praise God: Who is all-sufficient.

Confess: Any tendency to be greedy or dissatisfied with what God has provided for me.

Offer Thanks: To God, who is our all in all and releases us from bondage to greed.

Ask God: Dear all-sufficient Lord, I pray that my child would heed your warning to watch out and guard against all kinds of greed, because her life does not consist in the abundance of her possessions. She faces such great temptation to want the stuff that the world offers. I pray against the lies of the Enemy that she can't be happy unless she stockpiles material things. Gently teach her how to give up control and let you be the ruler of her life. Take away her desire to always want something more. Reveal to her the true source of her value and what an abundant life as your child is all about. I pray that she will manifest inner peace as she learns to delight herself in you and not in material things. In Jesus' name, amen.

Remember: God is all-sufficient for life and godliness.

Growing Strong through Endurance

When your faith is tested, your endurance has a chance to grow. So let it grow, for when your endurance is fully developed, you will be strong in character and ready for anything. (James 1:3–4 NLT 1996)

Praise God: Who is all-wise.

Confess: Any lack of commitment to endure whatever God deems necessary for me to grow in faith.

Offer Thanks: That God sanctifies us so that we will be prepared for anything!

Ask God: All-wise God, I pray that when you allow my child's faith to be tested, she will understand that her endurance has a chance to grow. Let it grow and develop fully so that she will be strong in character, ready for anything. As she faces difficult situations, may she find comfort in knowing that everything goes through your "love filter" first. Help her endure unpleasant, painful circumstances with confidence that even though she doesn't understand why you are allowing these trials in her life, she can trust you. Sustain her by your grace to endure difficulties without complaining, lashing out, or trying to escape them. May she persevere patiently so that she will not miss out on all the good you have planned for her. Use these trials to deepen her relationship with you and strengthen her trust in you. In Jesus' name, amen.

Remember: Our all-wise God sanctifies us through trials.

Involved in the Life of the Church

Let us consider how to stimulate one another to love and good deeds, not forsaking our own assembling together, as is the habit of some, but encouraging one another; and all the more as you see the day drawing near. (Hebrews 10:24–25 NASB)

Praise God: Who is our almighty Lord.

Confess: Any attitudes or habits that keep me from being involved in my church.

Offer Thanks: That God ordained the church for good deeds and the outpouring of his love.

Ask God: Almighty Lord, head of the church, I pray that my child will consider how to stimulate others to love and good deeds. I ask that he would not forsake assembling together with other believers, as is the habit of some, but will encourage others even more as he sees the day drawing near. Father, may he take this command to heart and be intentional about going to church. May he go expecting to hear from you and desiring to use his gifts to bless, encourage, and edify others. When he doesn't want to go because he thinks the teaching is boring or he has no friends, I ask that he would obey you. Help him learn that obedience always brings blessing. It delights your heart when the family of God comes together in unity and love, and I pray that throughout his life, my son will delight your heart. In Jesus' name, amen.

Remember: Almighty God ordained the church body to worship him together.

Having Clean Hands
and a Pure Heart

Who may ascend the hill of the LORD? Who may stand in his holy place? He who has clean hands and a pure heart, who does not lift up his soul to an idol or swear by what is false. He will receive blessing from the LORD. (Psalm 24:3–5)

Praise God: Who is holy.

Confess: The seemingly insignificant ways I come to God with hands that are not clean and a heart that is not pure.

Offer Thanks: That our holy God desires to bless his holy people.

Ask God: Most holy God, I ask that when my child ascends the hill of the Lord and stands in your holy place, she will have clean hands and a pure heart, not lifting up her soul to an idol or swearing by what is false. May she receive blessing from you. Thank you for saving her so that now and forever she stands with a pure heart in your eyes. O Lord, may she walk with you, seeking to have a clear conscience and clean hands so that her actions will be an extension of your hands reaching out to those who are lost or in desperate need. May her hands bring your touch of comfort and hope. May she have a pure heart, uncorrupted by the world and surrendered to your divine will. May she enjoy a life of spiritual blessing because of her walk with you. In Jesus' name, amen.

Remember: Our God is holy and loves to bless us.

Confidence in God's Guidance

Send forth your light and your truth, let them guide me. (Psalm 43:3)

Praise God: Who guides.

Confess: Any inclination to walk away from God's light and truth.

Offer Thanks: For the times God has guided me to the right path when I have not known which way to go.

Ask God: God who guides, send forth your light and your truth; let them guide my child. When his way seems clouded, I pray that his first recourse will be to read your Word and pray. Grant him faith to believe your promise that your Word is a lamp to his feet and a light to his path. May he be secure knowing that you love to shed your light if he will only ask. Give him faith to trust that you will reveal your light at the proper time for his next step. Increase his faith that you are with him, always ready to aid him, and enable him to carry out what you have shown him. I ask you to grant him courage and strength to be obedient even when your plan doesn't make sense. Please help him make it a daily habit to seek the light of your divine guidance that will diffuse the darkness around him. For your glory and his joy. In Jesus' name, amen.

Remember: God guides us by his light and truth.

Knowing God through Praise

Those who know your name will trust in you. (Psalm 9:10)

Praise God: Who is supreme.

Confess: Any lack of interest in wanting to know God fully and trust him completely.

Offer Thanks: For the fullness of our supreme God.

Ask God: O supreme Lord, the great I AM, I cry out for my child to know your name and thereby trust you. I ask you to thwart the lies of Satan as he tries to undermine her concept of who you are. May she diligently pursue knowing you by reading your Word and praising your attributes. May she come to know you as her rock, fortress, stronghold, deliverer, and shield in whom she can take refuge. May she come to trust you as gracious, compassionate, slow to anger, rich in love, faithful, righteous, and good to all. Teach her that offering praise to you is her greatest offensive weapon against Satan's attacks. For every need, problem, inadequacy, or trial she encounters, may praise for an attribute of your supreme character well up in her heart, giving her peace and strength to be victorious in the situation. May she be a woman of praise who blesses your holy name. In Jesus' name, amen.

Remember: God is supreme, worthy of our trust and praise.

Choose Entertainment Carefully

Whatever is true, whatever is noble, whatever is right, whatever is pure, whatever is lovely, whatever is admirable — if anything is excellent or praiseworthy — think about such things. (Philippians 4:8)

Praise God: For he is holy.

Confess: Any entertainment choices that are vile or worthless in God's sight.

Offer Thanks: That our holy God calls us to nurture pure hearts and minds.

Ask God: Holy Father, I pray that my child will choose whatever is true, whatever is noble, whatever is right, whatever is pure, whatever is lovely, and whatever is admirable. If anything is excellent or praiseworthy, may she think about such things. Protect her from the corrupting influence of entertainment that would lead her away from a godly mind-set. Guide her decisions and help her discern what is true, pure, and praiseworthy in what she reads, watches, and listens to. Give her strength to discipline not only her mind and heart but her time and resources in her entertainment choices. May she reject ungodly entertainment and instead choose media that teaches your truth, strengthens her faith, and encourages her spirit. May she take no part in the worthless deeds of darkness but seek to be a woman after your own heart. In Jesus' name, amen.

Remember: Our holy God wants us to focus our minds and hearts on whatever is excellent and true.

Using Social Media

Do not let any unwholesome talk come out of your mouths,
but only what is helpful for building others up according to their
needs, that it may benefit those who listen. (Ephesians 4:29)

Praise God: For he is kind.

Confess: Any habits of gossip or slander.

Offer Thanks: To God, whose words of grace and truth call us
into relationship with him.

Ask God: O kind Lord, I pray that my child will not let any
unwholesome talk come out of her mouth, but only what is
helpful for building others up according to their needs, that it
may benefit those who listen. I ask that your protective hand
would cover my daughter's relationships with friends and
schoolmates. Her social life is so important to her. Give me
wisdom in teaching her to set appropriate boundaries on the
content of social media and the amount of time she spends
on it. As she communicates with others, grant her a keen
awareness of the impact of her own behavior, and keep her
from getting caught up in gossip or any other behavior that
might harm others. When she receives inappropriate or illegal
content, give her wisdom to realize that it is wrong and take
the right actions to protect herself and defend others. Protect
her from receiving vile or demeaning images and messages.
I pray that she would be careful to use social media in a way
that honors you and builds others up. In Jesus' name, amen.

Remember: God wants us to build each other up in love.

For a Child Away from Home

The eyes of the LORD are on the righteous and his ears are attentive to their cry. (Psalm 34:15)

Praise God: Who is always watchful.

Confess: The times I feel that God has overlooked me and am tempted to believe that he doesn't care.

Offer Thanks: To God, who watches over the righteous and listens to their cries.

Ask God: O watchful Father, I am so grateful that your eyes are on my child, and your ears are attentive to her cry. She is far away from home, where I cannot see her, embrace her, or listen for her cries for help. I feel so helpless, but you, Lord, are always watchful, always listening. Help her believe that you hear her every prayer and will respond to her every need. I ask that she would not feel invisible to you or cut off from your protective care. Give her peace that because of your love for her, she can be confident of your watchful care. May she trust your promises that you will not let her foot slip and that you will keep her from harm, watching over her coming and going, now and forevermore. May she find great comfort in knowing that your eyes are always watching over her. In Jesus' name, amen.

Remember: Our God watches over us and always listens to our prayers.

Being a Leader Who Serves

Jesus told [his disciples], "In this world the kings and great men lord it over their people, yet they are called 'friends of the people.' But among you it will be different. Those who are the greatest among you should take the lowest rank, and the leader should be like a servant." (Luke 22:25–26 NLT)

Praise God: Who is a servant.

Confess: Any tendency to be an arrogant, demanding leader who lords it over others.

Offer Thanks: That God is a servant-leader, who shows by his example how true leaders serve others.

Ask God: Servant Lord, I pray that my child would not be like the kings and great men of this world who lord it over other people and call themselves "friends of the people." May he be different. If he is the greatest among others, I pray that he would take the lowest rank, and if he is a leader, may he be like a servant. You, Lord, have given him a gift of leadership and an opportunity to lead. I pray that he would recognize that this gift comes from your generous hand. I ask with all my heart that he would be a leader like Jesus, who was known for his goodness, strength of character, kindness, and servant heart. May my son come before you every day to learn how to lead as you would lead, with a servant heart. In Jesus' name, amen.

Remember: Jesus is the greatest servant-leader.

For Success in Life

In everything [David] did he had great success, because the LORD was with him. (1 Samuel 18:14)

Praise God: Who is gracious.

Confess: The times I desire success apart from the Lord.

Offer Thanks: That our gracious God blesses the righteous with success.

Ask God: Dear gracious Father, I pray that it will be said of my child, as it was of your servant David, that in everything he did he had great success, because the Lord was with him. Father, protect him from the pressures of the world that scream out that a man's value is in how successful he is. I pray that he will keep his priorities in order so that he will not be crushed under the burden of striving to succeed merely for material gain, social status, or the approval of others. May he never sacrifice his relationship with you by striving for acclaim and the world's applause. Lord, by your grace help him seek your kingdom first. Keep him from depending on his own gifts and strengths, and help him recognize that his adequacy comes from you. May he find great delight in honoring you as he pursues success as a man of integrity, faithfulness, peace, wisdom, kindness, excellence, and a pure heart in all he does. In Jesus' name I pray, amen.

Remember: God delights in being gracious to those who walk with him.

To Feed on God's Words

When your words came, I ate them; they were my joy and my heart's delight, for I bear your name, O LORD God Almighty. (Jeremiah 15:16)

Praise God: Who is the living Word.

Confess: The times I approach God's Word reluctantly, as if it is a duty rather than a joy and a delight.

Offer Thanks: That God has given us his Word to bring us joy and delight by feeding our hearts and minds with his life-giving truth.

Ask God: Blessed, living Word, may my child proclaim, "When your words came, I ate them; they were my joy and my heart's delight, for I bear your name, O Lord God Almighty!" Lord, your words are like no others. They give us life — abundantly and eternally. I ask that my child would know this and would choose to feed on your Word every day of his life. I ask that your Word would nourish his soul, train his mind, and guide him in all your ways. May your words bring hope to his heart, granting him strength for another day. I pray that he will experience the exceeding joy and great reward of being obedient to your Word. In Jesus' name, amen.

Remember: God is the living Word, given to nourish and delight us.

To Have and to Be
a Good Friend

Two are better than one, because they have a good return for their work: If one falls down, his friend can help him up. But pity the man who falls and has no one to help him up! (Ecclesiastes 4:9–10)

Praise God: Who is full of compassion.

Confess: The times I have not been a true friend who is willing to help a friend in need.

Offer Thanks: For the friends God has sent to come alongside and help me in my times of need.

Ask God: Compassionate Father, I ask that my child would rejoice in the truth that two are better than one, because they have a good return for their work. If one falls down, his friend can help him up. May he pity those who fall and have no one to help them up! I pray that my child will be a good friend who takes the time to love and support others. May he find a friend who shares his love for you, who desires to obey your commands and walk in your ways, and who responds to the needs of others with a compassionate heart like yours. May my son enjoy the companionship of such a friend all of his life. I ask for this gift of friendship in the name of Jesus, amen.

Remember: The heart of God is compassionate and loving, desiring that no one would struggle alone.

Trusting God
When Facing Terminal Illness

I cry out to God Most High, to God, who fulfills his purpose, for me.... Trust in the LORD with all your heart and lean not on your own understanding. (Psalm 57:2; Proverbs 3:5)

Praise God: Who is the Lord Most High.

Confess: The times I hesitate to trust the Lord with all my heart.

Offer Thanks: That the Lord God Most High is faithful to fulfill his purpose for me.

Ask God: I cry out to God Most High, to God, who fulfills his purpose for my child. May he trust in you with all his heart and not lean on his own understanding. I am asking for a lot, Lord, because my son's days on earth are coming to an end. I pray that during his remaining days, he will trust that your perfect purpose for his life is being fulfilled. In the midst of the pain, the unknown, and the fear, please manifest your unfailing love, care, and sweet comfort to his heart. Reveal to him that his life, even in this bed, brings you glory. May his faith in you shine on all who come in contact with him. When your appointed time comes to take him home, grant him your peace in knowing that Jesus has prepared a special place just for him in heaven. Thank you that you do not take the death of your saints lightly, nor will you take lightly the death of my son. That promise comforts my heart. May your will be done. In Jesus' name, amen.

Remember: God Most High can be trusted, even when we do not understand his ways.

Comfort after the Death of a Loved One

We prefer ... to be absent from the body and to be at home with the Lord. (2 Corinthians 5:8 NASB)

Praise God: Who is our comfort.

Confess: Any hardness of heart or unbelief that rejects the comfort God offers.

Offer Thanks: That our God of comfort gives us the hope of being in his presence forever.

Ask God: God of all comfort, I pray that my child will believe that to be absent from the body means to be at home with you. May this truth bring sweet comfort like a warm blanket over her heart. May she find solace in knowing that the moment her loved one closed his eyes on earth, he opened them in heaven, where he can see you face-to-face. Give her peace in knowing that the loving arms of Jesus welcome into his new eternal home every child of God who dies. May this give her true hope in the midst of her grief. Even though she doesn't understand why her loved one died, increase her faith to trust your heart. Console her with the remembrance that even Jesus cried after the death of Lazarus, someone he loved very much. Loving Father, you promise to mend the brokenhearted and heal those who mourn. I ask you to do both for my daughter. In Jesus' name, amen.

Remember: No loss is beyond the reach of God's healing comfort.

Live in the Light of Love

Whoever loves his brother lives in the light, and there is nothing
in him to make him stumble. But whoever hates his brother is
in the darkness and walks around in the darkness; he does not
know where he is going, because the darkness has blinded him.
(1 John 2:10–11)

Praise God: For he is light.

Confess: When I have stepped out of the light of God's love
and withheld it from others.

Offer Thanks: That God's forgiveness releases us from the dark
power of hate to walk in the light of his love.

Ask God: O blessed Light, I ask that my child would love his
brother and live in the light, where there is nothing to make
him stumble. Help him to see that if he hates his brother, he
is in the darkness and walks around in the darkness; he does
not know where he is going, because the darkness has blinded
him. Help him to remember that it is only by your love and
grace that his sins are forgiven, so help him to be quick to
forgive others. May he desire to have a clean heart before you.
Give him a heart that seeks your forgiveness for causing pain
to others. Please set his heart free from the hateful emotions
that are so easy to cling to when relationships are difficult.
May he walk freely in the light of your love and not in the
darkness of hate. In Jesus' name, amen.

Remember: The light of God's love sets us free from bondage
to darkness.

Be Faithful to Keep
and Teach the Ways of God

Love the LORD your God with all your heart and with all your soul
and with all your strength. These commandments that I give you
today are to be upon your hearts. Impress them on your children.
Talk about them when you sit at home and when you walk along
the road, when you lie down and when you get up.
(Deuteronomy 6:5–7)

Praise God: Who is our teacher.

Confess: Times I have neglected to impress God's Word on
the hearts of my children.

Offer Thanks: That God teaches us all we need for life and
godliness through his Word.

Ask God: O great Teacher, I pray that my child will love you
with all his heart, soul, and strength, and that your commandments will be on his heart so that he would impress them on
his children. I pray that he would talk about them with his
children when they sit at home and walk along the road, when
they lie down and get up. Give my son a passion to learn your
ways and obey your commands all the days of his life. May
he be a faithful student of your life-giving Word and teach it
diligently to his children so that succeeding generations of our
family will love and obey you. Grant us this legacy of faith for
your kingdom and glory. In Jesus' name, amen.

Remember: God loves his children and is faithful to each generation that does what is right and good in his sight.

Be Kind to Everyone

Make sure that nobody pays back wrong for wrong, but always
try to be kind to each other and to everyone else.
(1 Thessalonians 5:15)

Praise God: For he is kind.

Confess: The times I retaliate, even in small ways, against
those who have wronged me.

Offer Thanks: That God is no respecter of persons but wants
all people to be kind and to be treated kindly.

Ask God: O most kind Father, I ask that my child would not
pay back wrong for wrong but will always try to be kind to
everyone. Lord, so many girls express unkind and hurtful
comments about other girls — even their best friends. I pray
that you will protect my daughter from participating in this
unwholesome and potentially destructive habit. Fill her with
your loving Spirit so that whether she is with friends or strang-
ers, her kind words will bring encouragement and be a salve
to wounded, hurting hearts. May her kindness shine the light
of your love in dark places. In Jesus' name, amen.

Remember: God is kind and loving toward all he has created.

May God's Good Work Be Done!

[God] who began a good work in you will carry it on to completion until the day of Christ Jesus. (Philippians 1:6)

Praise God: For he is supreme.

Confess: The sin of unbelief.

Offer Thanks: That the supreme God of heaven and earth is working his plan in my child's life even though I can't see it.

Ask God: O supreme God, I pray that the good work you have begun in my child's life will be carried on to completion until the day of Christ Jesus. Thank you for the incredible hope that you are working in and through my son and have a purpose for his precious life. I pray that he would not fight you in the good work of his salvation but would be filled with such a deep, reverential fear of who you are that he would desire only to live out your perfect plan. Protect him from making decisions that would lead him astray. May he realize that his nearsighted, selfish plans could never measure up to your excellent eternal plan. May he, by the power of your Holy Spirit, choose the straight and narrow road that leads to carrying out the good work that you began when he asked you into his heart. Lord, it brings me great joy to know that the good work you began in his life will be carried to completion. Hallelujah! In Jesus' name, amen.

Remember: God reigns supreme and will complete his good work in us.

No Fear of Failure

I am the LORD, your God, who takes hold of your right hand and says to you, Do not fear; I will help you. (Isaiah 41:13)

Praise God: For the Lord is there.

Confess: When I allow the Enemy to strike fear in my heart and cause me to forget that my Lord is there to help.

Offer Thanks: That the Lord takes hold of my hand and drives away my fear.

Ask God: O Lord who is there, I pray that my child will know that you are his Lord, who takes hold of his right hand and says to him, "Do not fear; I will help you." Please help him realize that his fear of failure is a spiritual battle. Show him that the Enemy is using fear to immobilize and paralyze him, keeping him from experiencing a happy, fruitful life. I ask that you would help him take his eyes off himself and focus them on you, trusting you for all the help he needs. May his confidence grow as he believes your promise that no matter what he tries, how vulnerable he feels, or how scared he is, you are there holding his hand and helping him. Give him such a sense of your presence that his fears melt into faith. I ask in the name of Jesus that the spirit of fear be torn down and replaced with your spirit of power, love, and self-discipline. In Jesus' name, amen.

Remember: When God takes our right hand, we have all the help we need.

Fight for a Victorious Life

Everyone born of God overcomes the world. This is the victory
that has overcome the world, even our faith. (1 John 5:4)

Praise God: Who is our victor.

Confess: When I have been prone to wander from my faith.

Offer Thanks: That the Lord's banner over me is always love
and victory.

Ask God: O victorious Father, I pray that my child will live in
the victory of this truth: Everyone born of God overcomes the
world. This is the victory that has overcome the world, even
his faith. Deliver my son from the lies of Satan, who con-
stantly tries to convince him to distrust his God, to become
discouraged when his prayers go unanswered, and to give up
on following Christ. O Lord, put resolve in his heart to not
run from the battles he faces but to fight wholeheartedly the
good fight of faith. When he is prone to wander, help him look
to Christ and the overwhelming victory he won at the cross.
By the power of your Holy Spirit, fill him to live a victorious
life in Christ. Protect him from experiencing the tragic loss of
an unyielded life that is ineffective in your kingdom. In Jesus'
name I pray, amen.

Remember: God is our banner, our victor who has overcome
the world.

Correcting Defiant Behavior

They rejected my advice and paid no attention when I corrected them. That is why they must eat the bitter fruit of living their own way.... But all who listen to me will live in peace and safety, unafraid of harm. (Proverbs 1:30, 31, 33 NLT 1996)

Praise God: Who is just.

Confess: The ways in which I act out with a defiant, rebellious spirit.

Offer Thanks: That God is absolutely fair in all his ways.

Ask God: O just Father, I pray that my child will not reject your advice or refuse to pay attention when you correct him, so that he will not eat the bitter fruit of living his own way. May he listen to you so that he will live in peace and safety, unafraid of harm. His behavior is becoming more and more defiant. He refuses to obey and even reacts destructively. O Lord, deliver him from this behavior that harms him physically, mentally, emotionally, and spiritually. Humble his heart to repent of this sin. May he believe your promise that you are faithful and just, ready to forgive his sin and give him a fresh, new start. Please change his rebellious heart into a listening, obedient heart that enjoys the benefits of obedience: joy, no harm to himself or others, and no fear of correction. May he learn that when he is tempted to rebel, the power of the Holy Spirit living in him will help him do what is right if he asks for help. In Jesus' name, amen.

Remember: God is just, absolutely righteous, and always fair in everything he does.

To Experience God's Love
in the Midst of Divorce

I pray ... that Christ may dwell in your hearts through faith. And
I pray that you, being rooted and established in love, may have
power, together with all the saints, to grasp how wide and long
and high and deep is the love of Christ. (Ephesians 3:16–18)

Praise God: For his extravagant love.

Confess: Any attitudes or actions that may have contributed to
my divorce, as well as any lingering bitterness or anger.

Offer Thanks: For God's extravagant love that dwells in our
hearts by faith.

Ask God: O God of extravagant love, I pray that Christ may
dwell in my child's heart through faith, and that she would be
rooted and established in love. Grant her power, together with
all the saints, to grasp how wide and long and high and deep
is the love of Christ. Father, I entrust my child to your extravagant love and pray that she would experience it in a deeply
personal way. Like me, she has suffered deep pain from this
divorce and feels as if her world is falling apart. Loving God,
protect her tender heart during this difficult time. Comfort
her and help her know that none of this is her fault. Root her
so deeply in your love that nothing will shake her confidence
in you. Please break the cycle of divorce in this family and
enable us to live in peace with one another. In Jesus' name,
amen.

Remember: God's extravagant love gives us a strong foundation for living.

Adjusting to Life in a Blended Family

I can do everything with the help of Christ who gives me the strength I need. (Philippians 4:13 NLT 1996)

Praise God: For he is all-sufficient.

Confess: The times I contribute to chaos or disorder in my family.

Offer Thanks: That Christ is sufficient to help me do what seems impossible.

Ask God: All-sufficient God, I ask that my child would do everything with the help of Christ, who gives him the strength he needs. I ask that he would cling to this promise as he finds his place in his new blended family. The divorce and remarriage have turned his world upside down. Lord, may he know that you deeply love him and will help him deal with all he is going through. Grant him hope and peace in the midst of this storm. Help him turn to you as he sorts through his emotions and the hurts he holds inside. Give me wisdom to know how and when to reassure him of my love. I pray this prayer for any stepchildren as well. We all need your help and strength as we interact with one another. I pray that each of us will establish a healthy, respectful relationship with one another. Help us to treat each other in a way that brings you glory. In Jesus' name, amen.

Remember: God is sufficient for our every need.

For Being Single

Whom have I in heaven but you? And earth has nothing I desire besides you. My flesh and my heart may fail, but God is the strength of my heart and my portion forever. (Psalm 73:25–26)

Praise God: Who is all-sufficient.

Confess: When my own heart is not satisfied with God's sufficiency.

Offer Thanks: That God is sufficient to love us perfectly and forever.

Ask God: All-sufficient Father, may my daughter proclaim, "Whom have I in heaven but you? And earth has nothing I desire besides you. My flesh and my heart may fail, but you are the strength of my heart and my portion forever." O Lord, may she say, "If I have you, Lord Jesus, I have enough." I pray that you will use the pain and loneliness of being single at this time in her life to draw her closer to you. May she trust your heart to provide for all the important relationships in her life. May she find worth and fulfillment in you and bask in all the spiritual blessings you have given her in Christ. When her heart leans toward self-pity and complaining, may she choose to be content in you. Instead of feeling empty, may she be filled with the fullness of Christ and experience the joy and peace of your Spirit overflowing in her life. Lord, if singleness is your choice for her, I pray that she will totally consecrate herself to you and depend on you to be her whole strength and happiness. In Jesus' name, amen.

Remember: God is sufficient for our every need.

Guard against Compromise; Choose Alignments Carefully

Be very careful never to make a treaty with the people who live in the land where you are going. If you do, you will follow their evil ways and be trapped. (Exodus 34:12 NLT)

Praise God: Who is righteous.

Confess: Any inclination to align myself with people who reject God's ways.

Offer Thanks: That God, our righteous Father, cares for our well-being.

Ask God: Righteous Father, I pray that my child would be very careful never to make a treaty with the people who live in the land where he is going. If he does, he will follow their evil ways and be trapped. Lord, his school is the land he goes to every day. Please protect him from making choices that would compromise or weaken his faith. Help him live by his convictions and not align himself with those who would lead him off your righteous path. Anoint him to stand boldly in his faith and to be a godly leader who is not ashamed to align himself with other believers. Give him wisdom to recognize temptations that would seduce him and draw him away from you. By the power of your Holy Spirit, shield his heart and mind and strengthen him to resist the temptations of immorality, drugs, alcohol, pornography, vulgar language, disrespect, and philosophies that would undermine his faith. I pray for your righteousness to rain down on this land, his school. In Jesus' name, amen.

Remember: Our righteous Father does not want us to be trapped in unrighteousness.

Strength to Be Persecuted for Christ's Sake

Blessed are you when people insult you, persecute you and falsely say all kinds of evil against you because of me. Rejoice and be glad, because great is your reward in heaven. (Matthew 5:11–12)

Praise God: Who is our warrior.

Confess: When I fear being ridiculed or shunned if I share my faith.

Offer Thanks: That God, our warrior, has already won the battle against evil.

Ask God: Dear warrior God, bless my child when people insult him, persecute him, and falsely say all kinds of evil against him because of you. May he rejoice and be glad, because great is his reward in heaven. My son is growing up in a world that is hostile to the knowledge of Christ. Help him stand strong in what he believes, knowing that you will protect those who hold fast to you. Strengthen him by the truth that you are the warrior at his right hand, so that he will not be intimidated by those who attack, ridicule, or try to embarrass him because of his faith. I ask that he, like Shadrach, Meshach, and Abednego who would not bow down to worship other gods, will boldly choose to obey you rather than people. May he be uncompromisingly righteous, kind, wise, and compassionate in speaking the truth, and resolved in his convictions to suffer for Christ's sake. Bless him with joy. Encourage him that his reward will be great in heaven. In Jesus' name, amen.

Remember: God is our warrior, who stands at our right hand.

A Refuge and Strength
for Disasters

God is our refuge and strength, an ever-present help in trouble.
Therefore we will not fear, though the earth give way and the
mountains fall into the heart of the sea. (Psalm 46:1–2)

Praise God: Who is our refuge.

Confess: The fears that well up within me because I do not
depend on God in trouble.

Offer Thanks: That God promises to be our refuge, strength,
and help in times of trouble.

Ask God: O blessed God, my refuge, I pray that my child will
turn to you as her refuge and strength, an ever-present help in
trouble. May she not fear, though the earth give way and the
mountains fall into the heart of the sea. Lord, with news of so
many floods, fires, severe storms, earthquakes, tornadoes, and
hurricanes, my daughter is often fearful. She questions why
you let these disasters happen. I ask you to give her calm assurance that you, the creator and possessor of the entire universe,
are in control. May she trust that you see and care about everything that happens. Help her realize that you are a refuge
and ever-present help for those who have lost everything. May
she turn to you in prayer, asking you to strengthen the rescue
workers, comfort the injured and grieving, and save those who
do not know Christ. Give her confidence to know that her
prayers make a difference. Comfort her with the assurance
that she can trust you to bring good from any disaster because
you are a good God. In Jesus' name, amen.

Remember: Our heavenly Father is good, and we can trust
him to be a safe refuge.

Replacing Fear with Peace

Peace I leave with you; my peace I give you. I do not give to you as the world gives. Do not let your hearts be troubled and do not be afraid. (John 14:27)

Praise God: For his Son, Jesus, is our Prince of Peace.

Confess: The times my heart is filled with fear rather than peace.

Offer Thanks: That Jesus stands ready to deliver me and my child from all our fears.

Ask God: O Prince of Peace, I ask that my child would have faith that you leave peace with him, and that the peace you give him is unlike the peace the world gives. Do not let his heart be troubled, and do not let him be afraid. My heart is grieved to see him anxious and fearful about so many things. O Father, may these fears bring him to a place of prayer, asking you to give him peace. May he believe that you will answer his prayer and give him a calm heart and a serene mind. May he know that you are good and 100 percent trustworthy to replace his fears with your peace. In Jesus' name, amen.

Remember: Jesus is the Prince of Peace.

Responding to Bullying

When [God's people] cry out to the LORD because of their oppressors, he will send them a savior and defender, and he will rescue them. (Isaiah 19:20)

Praise God: Who is our defender.

Confess: My lack of forgiveness for those who have wronged me.

Offer Thanks: That God who defends us also cares deeply for those who come against me.

Ask God: O Lord my defender, I ask that my child would cry out to you because of her oppressors, knowing that you will send a savior and defender to rescue her. My heart is sickened to know that she is being bullied at school, and that despite her complaints, the behavior has not stopped. She is feeling so worthless and devalued because of the continued taunts. O Father, defend my child. Guard her from these attacks. Please rescue her. Send a teacher, a friend, somebody who will see this bullying as it happens and step in to stop the oppressor. As a result of this trial, I ask that you would develop in her a spirit of forgiveness and prayer for the bully. Grant her courage to stand up to that child, knowing that you are her defender, who cares about what is happening to her. In Jesus' name, amen.

Remember: God is our defender.

Guard against False Teaching

Don't let anyone lead you astray with empty philosophy and high-sounding nonsense that come from human thinking and from the evil powers of this world, and not from Christ. (Colossians 2:8 NLT 1996)

Praise God: Who is truth.

Confess: The times I listen to and take to heart the lies of the Enemy.

Offer Thanks: That God reveals his truth to me through his Word and his Spirit.

Ask God: God of all truth, I ask that my child would resist anyone who would lead him astray with empty philosophy and high-sounding nonsense that come from human thinking and the evil powers of this world, and not from Christ. I pray that you would give him spiritual understanding to be astute and discerning in the classroom. May he quickly recognize humanistic teachings for what they are. Protect his mind from empty, worthless teachings that would deceive him and lead him away from you and the blessings you have for his life. I ask that he would take every thought captive to the obedience of Christ. Give him a holy desire to search the Scriptures for your words of truth and life. In Jesus' name, amen.

Remember: God is truth and does not lie.

Confronting Hidden Sin

He who conceals his sins does not prosper, but whoever confesses and renounces them finds mercy. (Proverbs 28:13)

Praise God: For his great mercy.

Confess: Any sin that has robbed me of joy in my relationship with Christ.

Offer Thanks: That no matter how often we need to come to Christ in repentance, our merciful God will always forgive.

Ask God: O God of great mercy, may my daughter not conceal her sins, for she will not prosper if she continues in them. I ask that she would confess and renounce them and find mercy. I am devastated to learn that she is living a double life, doing things that are wrong and trying to hide her disobedience. Thank you for bringing what was in the darkness into the light. I ask you to prepare her heart to be humble and repentant when she is confronted with her sin. May she see that what she has done is contrary to your Word and is drawing her away from you and from our family. The enemy of her soul wants her to believe that her sin is no big deal. Lord, may she recognize and forsake this sin, receive your great mercy, and experience the joy of starting anew. In Jesus' name, amen.

Remember: Our merciful God welcomes every repentant child with open, loving arms.

Receiving God's Merciful Love

> But then God our Savior showed us his kindness and love. He saved us, not because of the good things we did, but because of his mercy. He washed away our sins and gave us a new life through the Holy Spirit. (Titus 3:4–5 NLT 1996)

Praise God: For he is merciful.

Confess: My tendencies to judge others and not show mercy.

Offer Thanks: That I did not have to do one thing to receive God's merciful salvation.

Ask God: O merciful God, I cry out for my child to see that God his Savior showed him kindness and love. You saved him not because of the good things he did, but because of your mercy. You washed away all his sin and gave him a new life through your Holy Spirit. O Lord, open his spiritual eyes to see how deep, passionate, and merciful your love is for him. You know how often he struggles to believe this truth because he does not forgive himself for his past sins. Help him accept your undeserved forgiveness that you give at no cost to him because of Christ's great kindness and sacrifice. Reveal to him that your forgiveness frees him from the guilt of sin. May he believe this truth by faith and live in the beauty of your forgiveness. In Jesus' name, amen.

Remember: God is merciful, not giving us what we deserve.

Adopted from Eternity Past

He predestined us to adoption as sons through Jesus Christ to Himself, according to the kind intention of His will.
(Ephesians 1:5 NASB)

Praise God: Our Abba Father.

Confess: The times I do not recognize my value as God's precious child.

Offer Thanks: That through God's great loving-kindness, he has adopted me as his child for all eternity.

Ask God: Dear Abba Father, thank you that you predestined my child to adoption as a son through Jesus Christ to yourself, according to the kind intention of your will. May he know you as his heavenly Daddy. I look to you to remove his fear of rejection and abandonment and replace it with a relationship of delight and intimate trust in you. Through your example of spiritual adoption, give him an understanding of how special his earthly adoption is. Help him to know in the deepest parts of his being that I see him as my very own child. Give him joy in understanding that before the foundation of the world, you decided to bring us together in an earthly family just as you have planned for us to be in your heavenly family. As his mom, may I demonstrate to him your marvelous, unconditional loving-kindness in ways he can understand. Enable him to feel fully loved and accepted in my family and yours. In Jesus' name, amen.

Remember: God our Daddy is loving and kind.

Wisdom for
a Special-Needs Child

If any of you lacks wisdom, he should ask God, who gives generously to all without finding fault, and it will be given to him. (James 1:5)

Praise God: Who is wise.

Confess: When I challenge God's wisdom in creating my child just the way he is.

Offer Thanks: For God's wisdom in creating my unique, special child, who reflects his glory.

Ask God: All-wise Father, on behalf of my child who lacks earthly wisdom, I ask for your wisdom. You give generously to all without finding fault, and I trust that you will give wisdom to him. Lord, I don't know if my child will ever be able to read your Word or understand what we try to teach him about you, so I pray for a heart of wisdom that comes from you, his creator. Give him a heart that is pure and peaceable. Through the many challenges he will face in life, please show him that you love and care for him. May he know that he is your unique, beautiful, and precious child, created for your glory. May he come to trust you as his friend and Savior, who will never leave him. May he know the joy of depending on you and glorifying you all of his life. In Jesus' name, amen.

Remember: God is wise beyond our comprehension.

Loving Care for a Special-Needs Child

Dear friends, since God so loved us, we also ought to love one
another. No one has ever seen God; but if we love one another,
God lives in us and his love is made complete in us.
(1 John 4:11–12)

Praise God: Who is love.

Confess: When I am less than loving to those around me.

Offer Thanks: That God lives in us and gives us the privilege
of expressing his great love to others.

Ask God: All-loving Father, since you so love my child who
has special needs, I pray that those who know you will also
love my child. No one has ever seen you, Father God, but
if we love one another, you live in us and your love is made
complete in us. Because of my child's great daily needs, I ask
for your loving care over all of her life. In the eyes of the world,
she appears to be weak, and to some an unnecessary burden,
but in your eyes, Lord, she is your beloved child, a precious
gift entrusted to our care. Keep our eyes and hearts open to
all she has to give us and teach us. I pray that you will reveal
the power of your love in her life. Surround her with family,
friends, and a loving church that embrace and include her.
And when I am taken from her, keep her in your care through
the gentle, compassionate hands of others who love you. In
Jesus' name, amen.

Remember: God loves us beyond what we can imagine.

Comfort for Having a Distant Earthly Father

I will be a Father to you, and you shall be My sons and daughters, says the LORD Almighty. (2 Corinthians 6:18 NKJV)

Praise God: Who is our Father.

Confess: The distance I allow in my relationship with my heavenly Father.

Offer Thanks: That God is my perfect, loving Father.

Ask God: Heavenly Father, my child deeply misses his father. I pray that my child will find comfort and value in your promise that you, Lord Almighty, will be a Father to him, and that he will be your son. Help him remember that when he received you into his heart, you gave him the right to become his son. Comfort his heart with the knowledge that you, his loving Father, will never leave him or forsake him. Give him faith to believe that you love him unconditionally, that you call him by name, and that your plans for him are to give him a future and a hope. May he delight in knowing that you rejoice over him with singing and keep close watch over him. Everywhere he goes and in everything he does, may he look up and say with confidence, "Dad, you're here!" May he draw ever closer to your loving heart, trusting you to hear and answer every one of his prayers. May you be more real to him than any earthly father could ever be. I ask this in Jesus' name, amen.

Remember: God our Father calls us his sons and daughters and will never abandon us.

Moving to a New Place

Forget the former things; do not dwell on the past. See, I am doing a new thing! Now it springs up; do you not perceive it? I am making a way in the desert and streams in the wasteland.... Do not be afraid. (Isaiah 43:18–19; 44:2)

Praise God: Who does not change.

Confess: Any fear that unwanted changes in my life mean that God's love and faithfulness to his promises have changed.

Offer Thanks: For the good things God has prepared for me when I least expect it.

Ask God: Unchanging Father, may my child find courage in your comforting words: "Forget the former things; do not dwell on the past. See, I am doing a new thing! Now it springs up; do you not perceive it? I am making a way in the desert and streams in the wasteland.... Do not be afraid." Lord, you know how hard this move is for my daughter. She is anxious and insecure about all the changes she's experiencing. Remind her that you are the one true constant in her life. Help her trust that you will be with her every moment and will help her adjust. May she accept your sovereign plan so that her heart and mind will be at peace in the midst of change. Draw her into a deeper relationship with you that casts out all her fear. Fill her with excitement as she anticipates the awesome things you have planned for her future. In Jesus' name, amen.

Remember: God does not change; he is the one constant we have in life.

To Be Free from the Burden of Worry

Casting the whole of your care [all your anxieties, all your worries, all your concerns, once and for all] on Him, for He cares for you affectionately and cares about you watchfully. (1 Peter 5:7 AMP)

Praise God: Who cares.

Confess: The times I hold on to my concerns and try to handle them myself instead of entrusting them to God's watchful care.

Offer Thanks: That God's love for me is so great, he cares about all of my concerns — my well-being, my family, our future.

Ask God: Caring heavenly Father, I pray that my child will cast the whole of her cares — all her anxieties, worries, and concerns once and for all — on you. May she know that you care for her affectionately and care about her watchfully. O Lord, I ask that her trust in you would grow with each burden she places in your care. By a simple, prayerful faith, may she give you the things that weigh heavily on her heart and cause her mind to be tortured with worry. Develop confidence in her that when she gives her anxieties to you, you will handle them perfectly. Help me to be a trusting and faithful example to her by casting my own worries on you as you care for me. May my daughter experience peace in her heart as she surrenders each of her burdens to you. In Jesus' name, amen.

Remember: God cares for us with watchful, deep affection.

For Perseverance

You need to persevere so that when you have done the will of
God, you will receive what he has promised. (Hebrews 10:36)

Praise God: Who sustains.

Confess: The times I fail to seek God's sustaining help when
I need to persevere.

Offer Thanks: That God stands by, ready to sustain us in every
circumstance.

Ask God: O my God who sustains, I pray that you will uphold
and support my child to persevere so that when he has done
your will, he will receive what you have promised. May your
sustaining grace help him to be steadfast in pursuing your
will through uncomfortable, difficult times. I pray that he will
not try to wiggle out of challenges but will seek your will and
strength to persevere through them. May he trust that by not
giving up, the best is yet to come — answers to prayer, a resolu-
tion to a problem, deliverance from a situation. I pray for him
to desire that your will be done, trusting you for the outcome.
For your glory, in Jesus' name, amen.

Remember: God sustains us and always delivers on his
promises.

Armed against the Devil's Schemes

Be strong in the Lord and in his mighty power. Put on the full armor of God so that you can take your stand against the devil's schemes. (Ephesians 6:10–11)

Praise God: Who is powerful.

Confess: My habit of relying on my own strength rather than on the strength of God.

Offer Thanks: That God wants me and my child to have everything we need to stand firm against the Enemy's schemes.

Ask God: All-powerful God, I ask that my child would be strong in the Lord and in his mighty power. May he put on the full armor of God so that he can take his stand against the Devil's schemes. I pray that he would know the importance of the spiritual armor you provide: the helmet of salvation, the breastplate of righteousness, the belt of truth, the shield of faith, feet fitted with the readiness that comes from the gospel of peace, and the sword of the Spirit. May he arm himself daily so that he would be protected from Satan's clever, crafty, cunning, scheming, deceptive, and destructive lies. Shield my child's heart and mind through the truth of your Word, for your name's sake. Make him a mighty warrior in the kingdom of light. In Jesus' name, amen.

Remember: God is powerful, stronger than any enemy we face.

Standing Firm
in the Will of God

Stand firm in all the will of God, mature and fully assured. (Colossians 4:12)

Praise God: Who is our rock.

Confess: The times I construct my own foundation, ignoring the dependable foundation of God my rock.

Offer Thanks: That I can depend on God to be a stable foundation for my life.

Ask God: O God my rock, I ask that my child would stand firm in your will, mature and fully assured. Lord, the world offers so many enticing substitutes that promise a good life, but they all crumble and turn to dust. So I pray that my child will stand firmly on the foundation of your Son, Christ, the solid Rock. Give her full assurance of her salvation and the knowledge that Jesus is her hope of heaven. Please help her choose daily to walk in a manner that identifies her life with your ways. May she increase in her knowledge of you, having a deeper love for your Word, a growing faith, and a greater love for others. May she grow into spiritual maturity, trusting you with every detail of her life. No matter what the world throws at her, may she be totally confident to stand firmly on the foundation of her faith, seeking to obey the whole will of God. In Jesus' name, amen.

Remember: God is our rock, our firm foundation.

Choosing the
Path of Righteousness

He guides me in paths of righteousness for his name's sake.
(Psalm 23:3)

Praise God: Who is our guide.

Confess: The times I choose my own selfish paths rather than the righteous paths that bring honor to God's name.

Offer Thanks: That we can count on God's guidance to find the life path that honors him.

Ask God: Lord who guides, I ask that you guide my child in paths of righteousness for your name's sake. The world offers so many different paths to take, and the Enemy wants to guide him in any direction that leads away from you. I know there will be times when my son will want to be his own guide and choose his own path. But please, Lord, by your grace and great love, keep him on your path. A path that is right. A path that brings abundant joy and hope. A path that honors you. Whatever it takes, hinder him from going down any path other than yours. And Father, I ask that he would bring many others with him on your path of righteousness. In Jesus' name, amen.

Remember: God guides us on his path according to his righteousness.

THIRTY-ONE SCRIPTURE
BLESSINGS FOR MY CHILDREN

God is good. He delights in showering his children with his good blessings. And he gives us the privilege and honor of blessing one another. When we give a blessing, we are asking for God's goodness and divine care to be active in a person's life through a specific situation or for a specific purpose. We find many such blessings throughout the Bible.

The very first blessing in the Bible came from the mouth of God when he blessed Adam and Eve, saying, "Be fruitful and increase in number; fill the earth and subdue it" (Genesis 1:28).

God also gave a blessing you might recognize for Aaron and his sons, Israel's priests, to use to bless the lives of the Israelites:

> The LORD bless you, and keep you;
> The LORD make His face shine on you,
> And be gracious to you;
> The LORD lift up His countenance on you,
> And give you peace. (Numbers 6:24–26 NASB)

One of the blessings in the Bible that is dearest to my heart is when Jesus "took the children in his arms, put his hands on them and blessed them" (Mark 10:16). What a beautiful picture Jesus gives us!

As mothers who belong to God's family, we have the privilege of not only praying for our children but blessing them as well. By blessing our children, we become conduits of the power of God's favor, goodness, and victory on them. These blessings not only impact our children today but for years — even generations — to come.

So I encourage you to look for opportunities each day to bless your precious children. It may work well for you to speak your blessings aloud before your children go to school, at bedtime, or before a meal. Whenever possible, bless each child separately, placing that child's name in the blessing. It is especially meaningful to hold your hand out to or over your child; to touch your child tenderly on the head, arm, or shoulder; or to embrace your child in your arms as you give your blessing.

To help you get started in this practice, I have chosen thirty-one Scripture passages — one for each day of the month — to bless your children. At the end of the month, you may repeat them or add new blessings.

What a great joy it is to pray over and bless our children with God's infinite, immutable Word. He promises that his Word "will not return to me empty, but will accomplish what I desire and achieve the purpose for which I sent it" (Isaiah 55:11).

May you see these powerful blessings fulfilled in your children's lives:

> *In the name of Jesus, I bless you, _____, to love the Lord your God with all your heart and with all your soul and with all your mind and with all your strength. [And to] love your neighbor as yourself. (Mark 12:30, 31)*

> *In the name of Jesus, may the LORD bless you, _____, and keep you; the LORD make His face shine on you, and be gracious to you; the LORD lift up His countenance on you, and give you peace. (Numbers 6:24–26 NASB)*

In the name of Jesus, I bless you, _____, to trust in the LORD *with all your heart and lean not on your own understanding; in all your ways acknowledge him, and he will make your paths straight. (Proverbs 3:5–6)*

In the name of Jesus, I bless you, _____. May the God of peace make you holy in every way, and may your whole spirit and soul and body be kept blameless until our Lord Jesus Christ comes again. (1 Thessalonians 5:23–24 NLT)

In the name of Jesus, I bless you, _____, to be on guard so that you will not be carried away by the errors of … wicked people and lose your own secure footing. Rather, … grow in the grace and knowledge of our Lord and Savior Jesus Christ. All glory to him, both now and forever! Amen. (2 Peter 3:17–18 NLT)

In the name of Jesus, I bless you, _____, to not get tired of doing what is good. At just the right time [you] will reap a harvest of blessing if [you] don't give up. (Galatians 6:9 NLT)

In the name of Jesus, I bless you, _____, that you may stand firm in all the will of God, mature and fully assured. (Colossians 4:12)

In the name of Jesus, I bless you, _____, to produce the fruit of the Holy Spirit in your life: love, joy, peace, patience, kindness, goodness, faithfulness, gentleness, and self-control. (Galatians 5:22–23 NLT)

In the name of Jesus, I bless you, _____, to trust in the LORD *[and] find new strength. [You] will soar high on wings like eagles. [You] will run and not grow weary. [You] will walk and not faint. (Isaiah 40:31 NLT)*

In the name of Jesus, I bless you, _____, to rejoice in the Lord always. I will say it again: Rejoice! (Philippians 4:4)

In the name of Jesus, I bless you, _____. Don't worry about anything; instead, pray about everything. Tell God what you need, and thank him for all he has done. (Philippians 4:6 NLT)

In the name of Jesus, I bless you, _____, to hide God's Word in your heart that you might not sin against him. (Psalm 119:11 NLT, adapted)

In the name of Jesus, I bless you, _____, that whatever you do or say, let it be as a representative of the Lord Jesus, all the while giving thanks through him to God the Father. (Colossians 3:17 NLT 1996)

In the name of Jesus, I bless you, _____, to be strong and courageous! Do not be afraid or discouraged. For the LORD your God is with you wherever you go. (Joshua 1:9 NLT)

In the name of Jesus, I bless you, _____. Let the favor of the Lord your God be upon you; and confirm for you the work of your hands; yes, confirm the work of your hands. (Psalm 90:17 NASB, adapted)

In the name of Jesus, I bless you, _____, for he will command his angels concerning you to guard you in all your ways. (Psalm 91:11)

In the name of Jesus, I bless you, _____. May you have no fear of bad news, because you confidently trust the LORD to care for you. (Psalm 112:7 NLT, adapted)

In the name of Jesus, I bless you, _____. The LORD himself watches over you! The LORD stands beside you as your protective shade. The sun will not harm you by day, nor the moon at night. The LORD keeps you from all harm and watches over your life. The LORD keeps watch over you as you come and go, both now and forever. (Psalm 121:5–8 NLT)

In the name of Jesus, I bless you, _____, to live a life of love…. Love is patient and kind. Love is not jealous or boastful or proud or rude. It does not demand its own way. It is not irritable, and it keeps no record of being wronged. *(Ephesians 5:2; 1 Corinthians 13:4–5 NLT)*

In the name of Jesus, I bless you, _____, to be quick to listen, slow to speak, and slow to get angry.*(James 1:19 NLT)*

In the name of Jesus, I bless you, _____, with this assurance from Jesus: "My sheep listen to my voice; I know them, and they follow me. I give them eternal life, and they will never perish. No one can snatch them away from me." *(John 10:27–28 NLT)*

In the name of Jesus, I bless you, _____, to delight yourself in the LORD and he will give you the desires of your heart. *(Psalm 37:4)*

In the name of Jesus, I bless you, _____, that whatever you do, whether in word or deed, do it all in the name of the Lord Jesus, giving thanks to God the Father through him. *(Colossians 3:17)*

In the name of Jesus, I bless you, _____, to be careful to live a blameless life … [to] lead a life of integrity … [to] refuse to look at anything vile and vulgar … [and to] not endure conceit and pride. *(Psalm 101:2, 3, 5 NLT)*

In the name of Jesus, I bless you, _____, to fulfill Jesus' command: "Go and make disciples of all nations, baptizing them in the name of the Father and of the Son and of the Holy Spirit, and teaching them to obey everything I have commanded you. And surely I am with you always, to the very end of the age." *(Matthew 28:19–20)*

In the name of Jesus, I bless you, _____, with Jesus' promise: "If you abide in Me, and My words abide in you, ask whatever you wish, and it will be done for you." (John 15:7 NASB)

In the name of Jesus I bless you, _____, for you did not choose [Christ], but [Christ] chose you and appointed you to go and bear fruit — fruit that will last.... For [you] are God's workmanship, created in Christ Jesus to do good works, which God prepared in advance for [you] to do. (John 15:16; Ephesians 2:10)

In the name of Jesus, I bless you, _____, that Christ will be more and more at home in your [heart] ... as you trust in him. May your roots go down deep into the soil of God's marvelous love. (Ephesians 3:17 NLT 1996)

In the name of Jesus, I bless you, _____, for God to fill you with the knowledge of his will through all spiritual wisdom and understanding ... in order that you may live a life worthy of the Lord and may please him in every way: bearing fruit in every good work, growing in the knowledge of God. (Colossians 1:9–10)

In the name of Jesus, I bless you, _____, to have a crown of beauty instead of ashes, to receive the oil of gladness instead of mourning, and a garment of praise instead of a spirit of despair [that you] will be called [an oak] of righteousness, a planting of the LORD for the display of his splendor. (Isaiah 61:3–4)

In the name of Jesus, I bless you, _____, to put on the full armor of God, so that when the day of evil comes, you may be able to stand your ground. Stand firm with the belt of truth, the breastplate of righteousness, feet fitted with the gospel of peace, the shield of faith, the helmet of salvation, and the sword of the Spirit. (Ephesians 6:13–17, adapted)

ACKNOWLEDGMENTS

Thank you, Ann Spangler, my agent, whom I admire. Without you, this book would not be.

Cindy Lambert, you bless me because of your vision to give moms a go-to book to help them pray God's will for the needs of their beloved children.

Thank you, Zondervan publishers, for continuing to partner with me in the ministry of Moms in Prayer and giving me the best of the best of your staff:

Sandra Vander Zicht — you bless me with your gracious servant leadership and your thoughtful, insightful recommendations.

Londa Alderink — you bless me with your encouragement and excitement for this project.

I am deeply grateful for Amanda and Stephen Sorenson. God truly blessed me with the most gracious, gifted, talented editors ever. You are an answer to prayer. Amanda, what a precious gift you were in editing these prayers. Your spiritual insights, great patience, and always loving encouragement were like a beautiful bouquet of flowers given to me every time I received an email from you, and all the hours we spent on the phone seeking the Lord's wisdom on how he would want me to pray his heart concerning each need. We were agreeing together — how powerful!

Jennifer Lonas — I am so grateful for your keen eye in the final editing of the book. It was a joy to work with you.

Bob Hudson — I am thankful that God chose you as senior editor. You took such good care over the whole process of the book from beginning to end and gave timely encouragement.

Thank you, Moms in Prayer board members and leaders in the USA and around the world, headquarters staff, my Grandmothers in Prayer group, friends, and my immediate and extended family. This book is a result of your intercessory prayers. You will never know how much I was carried by your prayers. I could not have done this book without each one of you. All glory to the Lord for his goodness in giving you to me. This truly is "our" book!

And to all the moms and grandmothers around the world who pray regularly in a Moms in Prayer group, I appreciate your faithful commitment to unite in prayer and lift up the needs of your children, grandchildren, and their schools.

index of prayers

The topics here are broadly separated into seven categories of a child's developmental needs: (1) Emotional Health, (2) Intellectual Development, (3) Physical Health, (4) Protection, (5) Social Maturity, (6) Spiritual Growth, and (7) Spiritual Warfare. It is organized in this way to make it easy for the mom to find a prayer that is appropriate for her child's need at the moment. Under each major topic will be a number of minor topics. At times a prayer will fit into more than one category. The numbers refer to the numbers of the prayers (1–183), not the page numbers.

Emotional Health

A Clear Conscience

Choosing Priorities Wisely

Comfort for a Broken Heart

Controlling Anger

Be Courageous

Physical Health

Spiritual Growth

An Invitation from Fern

I would like to personally invite you to join a Moms in Prayer group or start one for mothers in your area.

Women who participate in Moms in Prayer recognize that our children live in immoral times and desperately need Jesus. We know that our schools are in crisis. And we take seriously Jesus' words that if two or more come together in his name and agree in prayer, he will answer.

Therefore, we come together to pray for one another's children and the schools they attend. We are committed to establishing a loving, supportive, and confidential atmosphere in which we stand together and pray according to the promises of God's Word. Our faith, hope, and peace grow ever stronger as we unite our hearts together in prayer and see God's power at work in our lives and the lives of our children.

Moms in Prayer is an international prayer movement of mothers who stand in the gap to pray for the lives of their children and the schools they attend. We are active in more than 140 nations, bringing mothers of diverse cultures and languages together to impact children and schools for Christ through united prayer. Our vision is for this generation of children and every school in the world to be covered with prayer.

To find a Moms in Prayer group in your area or to obtain information about how to start one, please contact us at www. MomsInPrayer.org or call 1-800-949-MOMS.

Arise, cry out in the night, at the beginning of the night watches! Pour out your heart like water before the presence of the Lord! Lift your hands to him for the lives of your children, who faint for hunger at the head of every street. (Lamentations 2:19 ESV)